THE MAKING OF A Mom

Practical Help for **Purposeful** Parenting

STEPHANIE SHOTT

Revell

a division of Baker Publishing Group
Grand Rapids, Michigan

Published by Revell
A division of Baker Publishing Group
P.O. Box 6287, Grand Rapids, MI 49516-6287
www.revellbooks.com

Printed in the United States of America

Library of Congress Cataloging-in-Publication Data is on file
at the Library of Congress, Washington, DC.

14 15 16 17 18 19 20 | 7 6 5 4 3 2 1

This book is packed with Scripture, prayers for our children and real-world advice to help moms raise godly kids. *The Making of A Mom* is a beautiful model of Titus 2 mentoring. If I could place this book in the hands of every new mother, I would.

LYNN DONOVAN
Author, *Winning Him Without Words* and *Not Alone*

Packed with wisdom and spiritual insight, *The Making of a Mom* helps women parent intentionally with God's purposes in mind. Plus, this book is flexible enough to be used individually, in a mentoring relationship or with a group.

KATHY HOWARD
Christian Speaker and Author of 6 Books, including *Unshakeable Faith*

The Making of a Mom is an exciting new book for all moms that also helps the Church put Titus 2:4-5 into action. Whether you're in the middle of motherhood, your children now have families of their own, or you're still thinking and praying about motherhood, this is the book for you!

KATHI MACIAS
Award-winning Author, *Mothers of the Bible Speak to Mothers of Today*
www.kathimacias.com

The Making of a Mom addresses the dreaded word so many Christians fear: mentor. Am I good enough to mentor someone? Do I know enough Scripture? What do I have to offer? Each one of us is called to be about our Father's business making disciples, helping others know the Father we love. I love what God is doing through The M.O.M. Initiative and Stephanie Shott.

JENNIFER MAGGIO
Author and CEO, The Life of a Single Mom Ministries

Packed with compelling stories, *The Making of a Mom* covers the full spectrum of what mothering with grace and love looks like. Not just grace for our children, but for ourselves Even grandmothers and mentors will find Stephanie's book an invaluable resource to encourage and inspire the mothers they are blessed to walk beside.

DINEEN MILLER
Author, *Not Alone*, *Winning Him Without Words* and *The Soul Saver*

The Making of a Mom will help you evaluate how you parent and how you *want* to parent. Full of wisdom, moms can find real answers for the challenges they face today in these pages.

ARLENE PELLICANE
Author, *31 Days to Becoming a Happy Wife*

Where was *The Making of a Mom* when I was raising five kids? I love that Stephanie doesn't heap on a big, fat load of "if you would just be a better person, a better mother, blah, blah, blah . . ." *The Making of a Mom* helps us all chuck the guilt, understand God's deep and unshakeable love, and encourage us to pass that love along.

RHONDA RHEA
Humor Columnist, TV Host and Author of 11 Books, including *Espresso Your Faith* and *Join the Insanity*

Stephanie Shott writes from a wealth of experience, sharing true stories and biblical principles. Mom's, you have a calling. *The Making of a Mom* will help equip and encourage you in yours!

DAVE STONE
Pastor, Southeast Christian Church
Author, *Faithful Families* series

In the *Making of a Mom*, Stephanie Shott mentors moms with her characteristic compassion and empathy. Offering practical tips, loving encouragement and God's wise counsel, Stephanie equips mothers to be godly mamas. I wish there had been a book like this when I was a single mom; I might have avoided so many pitfalls.

JANET THOMPSON
Speaker and Author of 17 Books, including *Woman to Woman Mentoring* and *Praying for Your Prodigal Daughter*, www.womatowomanmentoring.com

As you pore over *The Making of a Mom*, Stephanie's heartfelt words will move you. Her practical methods will help you be a better mom and mentor. We don't have to do this "mom thing" alone—let's encourage each other. We can start by reading, and then using, *The Making of a Mom*.

LORI WILDENBERG
Cofounder, 1 Corinthians 13 Parenting, Speaker, Licensed Parent and Family Educator
Coauthor, *Raising Little Kids with Big Love* and *Raising Big Kids with Supernatural Love*

Stephanie Shott's book, *The Making of a Mom*, is a must-have! Chock full of love and wisdom, she addresses everything from the loneliness of motherhood to parenting on your knees. This is a great resource for the expectant mom, the mom with a house full of kids and the experienced mom who is sharing life with a younger mom.

DEBBIE TAYLOR WILLIAMS
Speaker and Author, *The Plan A MOM in a Plan B World*

CONTENTS

FOREWORD

BY TRACEY EYSTER

If little girls are made of sugar and spice and everything nice, what might loving moms be made of? Moms are sweet and spicy, with lots of nice and a bit of sassy—but those descriptors don't provide a clear picture. Let's face it, every facet of being a mom is far more complicated than mere words can capture. Mom, you are God's one of kind masterpiece!

The grand assignment of motherhood is a noble, mandated role and moms need encouragement and a better understanding of God's design and desire for their lives.

What a breath of fresh air to have a seasoned mom, full of wisdom openly and candidly share her good, bad . . . and worst. In *The Making of a Mom* Stephanie Shott vulnerably shares what she has learned through motherhood—she cheers the rest of us on in our travels and encourages us to do the same for others. There are few like her who are willing to open up their lives to offer a well-laid-out map to those coming along the narrow path behind them. But that's exactly what Stephanie does as she shares valuable experiences in her life, and the lives of those she has been called to minister to for over two decades.

Stephanie challenges moms to have a clear understanding of who their kids are and provides practical suggestions on how to train them up in the way they should go. More importantly she reminds us all *whose* our kids are and that we are to passionately, intentionally and selflessly pour into their lives and launch them confidently into the forever care of their heavenly Father.

The blessing of motherhood brings with it a complex inter-twining of joy and angst—as we revel in the gift of molding a life and tremble at the prospect of getting it wrong. A mother's body, mind and heart gets pulled and tugged in many directions and in the tussling we, sadly, are sometimes far too hard on ourselves.

Stephanie has some great news for you, the truth that an abiding relationship with the One who knows you like no other can calm the tumult.

Only the One, who chose you to be the mom to those He entrusted to you, can keep you content and filled with peace. This heartfelt written journey with Stephanie will guide and equip you to be the mom God intended with grace and confidence, and to share that grace with other moms who can benefit from what you have learned.

Enjoy the journey.

Living for Him,
Tracey Eyster
Founder MomLifeToday.com and MomLifeBootCamp.com
Author, *Be the Mom* and Coauthor, *Beautiful Mess*
Cohost, Encouragement Cafe

INTRODUCTION

I saw her walking across the parking lot. She looked to be about 16 years old. Young in years, but great with child, she waddled past our car.

Memories of my own teen pregnancy flashed through my mind and I couldn't help but wonder if she was ready for the long road of motherhood ahead. Did she grasp the greatness of her new-found role in life? Did she understand how everything she had ever known in life was about to change? Did she have someone who would help her along the way or was this a journey she was going to travel alone?

She hesitated for just a quick second, turned her head away from me, lit a cigarette and then battled the wind, hair whipping around her face, as she continued to walk away.

My heart sank. "Lord, does she understand that her actions no longer affect just her body? Does she realize that her choices affect that little life within? Would she be willing to quit smoking if she knew the damage it could do to her baby? Lord, why doesn't she understand?"

And then it happened. The voice. Oh, it wasn't audible, but it was just as real as if it were. It was loud. It was clear. And it was powerful: "Because you're not teaching her!"

Perhaps it was a combination of things that had culminated in my calling—I'm not sure—but by the time my husband got back to the car, *The Making of a Mom* and the M.O.M. Initiative had been conceived in my heart and I had jotted down the outline for the book you are now holding in your hands. At a gas station. Such a strange place for the birth of a ministry, but that's exactly where this book and The M.O.M. Initiative were born.

When I was a young mom, I longed for a mentor, yet wondered why I could never seem to find one. I had just turned 18 when my son was born and I didn't have a clue what it meant to be a mom.

Oh, I thought I did. In fact, I thought the whole mom thing was going to be a breeze. I quickly learned that my dream of mother- hood was very different than the reality of motherhood.

I was young, without Christ, without a mentor and without a clue. I thought I was going to be the mom who did the right things, said the right things, never yelled at her kids, and loved playing Legos with them. I would bake my own bread and we would spend hours on end creating crafts and playing games together.

But that's not what happened. I soon became a divorced teen mom who felt the weight of the world on her shoulders. Somehow, the mom I wanted to be—the mom I thought I was going to be—got lost in the never-ending realities of motherhood as I worked two jobs to keep a roof over our heads and food on the table. It's pretty hard to be all and do all when you're really just overwhelmed by it all.

As the years passed, I married again, and not long after that I became a Christian. Everything changed, except that I still didn't have a mentor and I barely had a clue.

Motherhood was pretty messy for me. Everything seemed like an experiment and my kids were the guinea pigs. I tried a hodge- podge of parenting techniques touted by experts to be the solution to all my parenting faux pas. Some were helpful. Others left me wondering if those experts had children of their own.

That was 25 years ago and as I reflect back on the seasons of my life and the way I muddled through motherhood, I can't help but wonder where all the mentors were. I remember looking up to several women in the church, but for some reason I was never able to wiggle my way under their wings.

It shouldn't have been that hard. After all, mentoring is what we're called to do. It's a God-given way to leave a legacy of faith for those who come behind us, and it's also a powerful tool to help us reach our communities and this culture for the Lord Jesus Christ. I asked myself, *Could God possibly be calling me to minister to young mothers whose mom journey was much like mine? Could I really develop a dual-purpose resource that would help those moms outside the church navi- gate the difficult waters of motherhood, and could that same resource still be used as a tool to mentor moms within the church?* I didn't want to write the kind of book that makes a mom feel as if there was no way she could ever be a perfect mom. I wanted the book to be written by a mom who knows what it's like to blow it and then feel that she's one step away from messing up her kids for life.

Could I create a mentoring ministry that was also missional? A ministry that would reach out to moms beyond the four walls of the local church with the goal of leading them to Christ and at the same time minister to the hearts of moms who already know Him? Could this ministry help weave mentoring into the fabric of the local church and connect these churches with other ministries as well as with the community? Wow! What an impact we could have on our communities and this culture for Christ through the power of missional mentoring! I didn't know how, when or where, but I knew God was calling me to something much bigger than myself, and the thought of it left me shaking in my shoes!

It sounds a bit crazy, I know, but that's how it began—in the parking lot of a gas station when a young pregnant girl, who reminded me of myself, walked past me and lit up a cigarette. It was there that the Lord led me to minister to moms, to write *The Making of a Mom* and eventually to write a series of books uniquely designed with carefully crafted questions at the end of each chapter that would serve as a catalyst for conversation between group leaders and mentees. What if I could develop something that would enable women to have the confidence and courage to enter into a mentor/mentee relationship? What if I could provide a resource that would answer the questions every would-be mentor and small-group leader asks herself: *What do I say? What do I do? What do I use?*

That's when the Lord led me to launch a comprehensive ministry to help the Body of Christ make mentoring missional.

Sweet mom, I know we have never met, but I feel we were introduced that day at the gas station when *The Making of a Mom* was conceived and The M.O.M. Initiative was born. So, this is for all of you. Whether you're a new mom, a mom to teens, or a mom-to-be, *The Making of a Mom* is for those who feel alone in their journey, for those who wonder why the mother they thought they'd be doesn't look anything like the mother they've become in real life. It's a book for the mom who is afraid she's messing up her kids and doesn't have a clue what to do next. It's for the mom who feels she can't measure up and wonders if she'll ever be the perfect mom. It's for the courageous mom who is ready to take her motherhood journey to the next level. It's for those who are looking for a fresh biblical perspective on motherhood from someone who is willing to share her flaws and failures. It's from someone who knows how hard your journey is and who doesn't gloss over it and make you feel like being a mother is easy. It's for the new or expecting mom who really wants to become grounded in her understanding of what a mother is and what a mother does from a biblical perspective. This is for you, sweet mom. The one who loves her kids like crazy but is weary, worn out, and overwhelmed. The one who thinks she has to do it alone, yet knows there's no way she can.

And this book is for you, sweet mentor and ministry leader—those of you who have longed to weave mentoring into the fabric of your church or ministry but have felt you lacked the resources and support to get started. It's for those who are looking for a way to connect with moms in your church or your ministry and begin making a difference in their lives through mentoring. It's for those who want to start a ministry or small group for single moms, and for those who are ready to impact your community and this culture for the Lord Jesus Christ through the power of mentoring. It's for those of you who long to help women step into their Titus 2 shoes and fulfill their calling—who have been looking for tools to eliminate the awkwardness a mentor often feels when she isn't sure where to begin or what to say. It's for those of you who realize that we are at a crossroads in our culture and that if we reach the moms of this generation, then we will reach the heart of the next generation—but if we don't, we might lose them all.

In the back of this book, you will find Planning Guides for a variety of venues to help you start a M.O.M. Group and be on your way to making mentoring missional. There are also resources online at www.themominitiative.com to help you on your journey.

The Making of a Mom is not just a book to help moms know they are not alone; it's also a resource for the church so that moms won't have to be alone. As you open the pages of *The Making of a Mom*, you are about to venture into some familiar and maybe not-so-familiar territory—the deep places of a mother's heart where we discover there's so much more to us than we ever realized. There, in a mother's heart, is the place where we long for our children to become all God created them to be. But because we are plagued with all our own flaws and failures, we wonder if we are *enough* to get them there. We know God calls us to build character in our kids, but we struggle with how defective our own character is. There, in the deep places of a mom's heart, is where we know we love our children like crazy, but we're not even sure we love them well. We are mothers who try so hard to be strong yet realize the mom journey is the one journey we don't want to mess up. So, we rise from the rubble of our own insecurities and quietly confess, "I can't do this alone."

This book is for you, sweet mom! You're a heart molder—a world changer. You are more courageous than you ever thought you were and stronger than you give yourself credit for. You can do this mom thing, but you don't have to do it alone. I have been there and done that and I know *alone* makes motherhood even more difficult than it already is.

So, let's do this thing together—you, the mentors, the small-group leaders, the mentees and me. Let us lock our hearts and hands to raise the next generation for the glory of God. He has gifted us moms with extraordinary influence and we are definitely better together.

Oh, and by the way, I thought you should know that you have been the object of my prayers for a very long time. You still are. I pray that you will know the height and depth of God's love for you and your children. I pray that your heart will be encouraged as you realize that God partners with you in parenting your children. I pray that you will embrace the truth and the beauty of knowing that God has uniquely created and called you to be the mother of your children. I pray that the Lord does exceedingly abundantly above all you could ask or think. I pray that your entire family will come to know Christ and embrace His plan and purpose for their lives. And I pray that you will find a mentor to help you make the most of every minute of your mom journey, to embrace your God-given role and to inspire you to grasp the power of your influence, not only in your children's lives, but also for generations to come. ❀

Eternally His!
Stephanie Shott

1

NOT ALONE

As iron sharpens iron, so one person sharpens another.
PROVERBS 27:17

Alone. It is one of the biggest struggles busy mothers face. But we don't have to do the mom thing alone. In fact, we weren't meant to do any part of life alone. In "Not Alone," you will discover why other mothers feel the same way you do and how you can find freedom in the beauty of community with other moms. Some are modern-day moms, and others have already blazed the motherhood trail before us.

A Familiar Look

There she was, inching her way forward in the grocery line, clinging to the back side of her baby's pacifier with her teeth as she plunged her hand back and forth between her purse and her diaper bag. She was frantically searching for her wallet while trying to quiet one very loud and discontented toddler and at the same time attend to her crying infant.

I know the look. I've worn it too. I saw it in her eyes that day. Weary. Worn out. Frazzled. Unsure if she would ever get the mom thing down. Uncertain about how to handle her cranky kids. Wondering if one day she might be able to use the bathroom without interruptions. And then there was the fear that she might fall asleep in church because her toddler pulled an all night cry-a-thon.

She was one of so many moms who find themselves getting lost somewhere between the mounting pile of laundry and the dried spaghetti sauce in the carpet. She was like you. She was like me. She was like every mom on the planet—trying to figure it all out and wondering if she ever will. Look around, sweet mom, they are everywhere—moms just like you.

You may be a single mom who feels the weight of the world is on your shoulders. Or you may be married, but still feel as if you are sinking under the tidal wave of mommy-hood. You may be a widow who has lost the love of your life and is parenting alone, or you may be married to a husband who, for some reason or another, is completely out of the parenting picture.

You may be struggling to put the next meal on the table, or you may be a mother who has never had to suffer financial need. You may be escaping an abusive situation, or perhaps you're a mother who is still held captive by it. Maybe you are a mom who deals daily with a chronic, life-threatening or terminal illness, or perhaps you are caught up in the cycle of continually trying to figure out how to mother a child with special needs.

Moms, there are lots of them and they are everywhere. Yet, so often they feel isolated . . . alone . . . lonely, even in a house brimming with kids.

Kim's Story

Kim is happily married with four boys under the age of five. She is a stay-at-home mom whose house is full, whose days are hectic, and who struggles with feeling alone. Every trip to the store is a chore and a day at the park is impossible. She loves her children and she loves being a mom, but that doesn't make it easy. Being a mom seldom is.

As Kim makes her way through church on the way to the nursery, she scans the room. She can't help but notice the other moms. Their daughters are neatly dressed with matching ribbons in their hair. Their sons are quiet and well-behaved with what appears to be halos hovering above their heads.

Kim wonders if she could ever be *that* kind of a mom. You know, the mom who has all the right answers, doesn't raise her voice and never has to count to three. Would her boys ever promenade calmly through church, marching in a row like little soldiers? Could she possibly ever hold a conversation without being interrupted and feeling she must apologize for her children?

She feels alone—as if she is the only mom who struggles with shrieking boys, temper tantrums in the candy aisle, and random burping contests in the waiting room at the doctor's office. Comparing herself to the moms who seem to have it all together often leaves her feeling she can never measure up.

Her husband is a pastor and certain expectations come with being a pastor's wife. She's supposed to be the one who has it all together. Her kids are supposed to be the ones who wear halos. Kim's life doesn't look much like she thought it would. Oh, perhaps from the outside it seems to be a Pinterest-perfect home and Pinterest-perfect life. There is the adorably adorned house with the double car garage. There is the godly husband, the wife who loves her man. And, to top it off, there are two parents who cherish their children and work hard trying to raise them well.

Kim is a mom just like you and me. Feeling alone, inadequate, invisible and intimidated. She is afraid she won't parent her kids well—that she won't always do or say the right things and that her children will be messed up by her inadequacies. She fears for her sons' futures and wonders if they will turn out okay. Will they grow up to be men of character—men who love God and their wives? Will they raise their children well? Expectations run pretty high for a pastor's family.

What about their education? Kim's heart is telling her to homeschool her boys, yet etched deep within her soul are the words, "I'm not enough."

And their safety? What about their safety? It's a dangerous world out there and four boys in one household is a recipe for skinned knees, broken bones and a plethora of trips to the emergency room. She shudders at the thought of how many times she will have to pull an all-nighter at the E.R. while raising these rambunctious boys.

Like you, Kim is a mom who wishes she had a few more arms and a few more hours in her day. She longs for adult conversation, enough money to go out to eat, a full night's sleep and a long, hot, uninterrupted bath. With four boys tugging at her heart, she knows hers is a 24/7 gig that will often leave her weary, worn out and overwhelmed—but Kim wouldn't trade her life as a mom for all the world, even on the days she feels she isn't worthy to be a mom and is blowing it with her boys.

Today, as you are reading this, remember that there are millions of moms around the world. Their circumstances may be different from yours, but their hearts are the same. You're not alone! There are a myriad of moms whose hearts are overwhelmed and whose lives are filled with sticky Nutella fingertips and teens who think it's cool to talk back. They're moms just like you. Yet, like Kim, they wouldn't trade any of it for the world. And neither would you.

Community of Women

It doesn't have to be as hard as we make it sometimes. We weren't meant to make the mom journey alone. We don't have to trudge through motherhood on our own when help is only a phone call or text message away.

Threaded throughout Scripture is the concept of community among women—a sisterhood of sorts. Tucked oh so sweetly in the pages of Scripture, we find women who walked through life together. Some were friends, others were relatives; all needed each other.

Ecclesiastes 4:9-10 (*NIV*) tells us, "Two are better than one, because they have a good return for their labor: If either of them falls down, one can help the other up. But pity anyone who falls and has no one to help them up."

Naomi and Ruth

We look at stories like that of Naomi and Ruth and we find an unusual relationship of community. Both were widowed. Both loved and respected each other. Naomi was not only Ruth's mother-in-law, but also she was her mentor and friend.

Let's take a minute and pull back the curtain on this timeless relationship as we look at the discourse between Naomi, Orpah and Ruth after the loss of their husbands. Keep in mind that Orpah and Ruth may have lost their men, but Naomi had lost her husband and both of her sons:

> When Naomi heard in Moab that the LORD had come to the aid of his people by providing food for them, she and her daughters-in-law prepared to return home from there. With her two daughters-in-law she left the place where she had been living and set out on the road that would take them back to the land of Judah. Then Naomi said to her two daughters-in-law, "Go back, each of you, to your mother's home. May the LORD show you kindness, as you have shown kindness to your dead husbands and to me. May the LORD grant that each of you will find rest in the home of another husband." Then she kissed them goodbye and they wept aloud and said to her, "We will go back with you to your people." But Naomi said, "Return home, my daughters. Why would you come with me? Am I going to have any more sons, who could become your husbands? Return home, my daughters; I am too old to have another husband. Even if I thought there was still hope for me—even if I had a husband tonight and then gave birth to sons—would you wait until they grew up? Would you remain unmarried for them? No, my daughters. It is more bitter for me than for you, because the LORD's hand has turned against me!" At this they wept aloud again. Then Orpah kissed her mother-in-law goodbye, but Ruth clung to her. "Look," said Naomi, "your sister-in-law is going back to her people and her gods. Go back with her." But Ruth replied, "Don't urge me to leave you or to turn back from you. Where you go I will go, and where you stay I will stay. Your people will be my people and your God my God. Where you die I will die, and there I will be buried. May the LORD deal with me, be it ever so severely, if even death separates you and me." When Naomi realized that Ruth was determined to go with her, she stopped urging her (Ruth 1:6-18, *NIV*).

It's a story that grips your heart. Such great loss. Such a huge decision to make—to go with Naomi or stay where life was familiar and a future husband would be more probable. Orpah stayed; Ruth went. She loved her mother-in-law too much to remain in the only land she had ever called home. Ruth clung to Naomi and to a future that held little promise. They had a powerful relationship that was strengthened by Ruth's devotion to her mother-in-law and solidified by both women's devotion to God.

After making the treacherous trip to Bethlehem, they entered the land of hope with very little hope of their own. They were widows with nothing but each other. Many of the people recognized Naomi. After all, Bethlehem was her hometown. When she overheard them whispering to one another, "Is this Naomi?" she was quick to let them know she wasn't the same woman who had left years ago. "Naomi" means "delight," but now, coming home empty-handed and broken-hearted left her feeling anything but delightful.

"Don't call me Naomi," she responded. "Instead, call me Mara [bitter], for the Almighty has made life very bitter for me. I went away full, but the Lord has brought me home empty. Why call me Naomi when the Lord has caused me to suffer and the Almighty has sent such tragedy upon me?" (Ruth 1:20-21, *NLT*).

As a grieving widow who was also grieving the loss of both of her sons, Naomi wasn't exactly in the best state of mind to be good mentor material. Ruth, however, looked beyond her pain and recognized a faith that even Naomi had struggled to find. Naomi didn't always get it right. Her deep sorrow certainly didn't make her the most pleasant woman on the planet. Yet somehow, somewhere along the way, Naomi must have left a trail of faith worth following. Why else would Ruth be so determined not only to follow her, but also to follow her God? Somewhere, beyond the written Word, was a life worth following—a life of faith in a God who is faithful even when circumstances are difficult.

When Ruth married Naomi's son, she may not have been able to choose her mother-in-law, but when she lost him, she was able to choose her mentor. She chose Naomi. Perhaps Naomi had been mentoring Ruth all along. Maybe Ruth clung to Naomi because years at Naomi's side had taught her what life, love and everything in between was all about. Maybe she overheard Naomi's prayers as she sought God's face for her sons. Could it have been that Naomi shared how wonderful her God was while they were baking bread and making meals together? Perhaps she unfolded stories of Yahweh's faithfulness while they sat side by side folding clothes.

We don't really know much about their lives before they took this journey together, but we know that while they may have felt they had lost it all, they still had each other, and that made all the difference in the world. The road ahead would definitely be a rough one, but a tough journey together is always a bit easier than a bumpy ride alone.

So much has changed since the days when women surrounded themselves with other women. We live very independent lives, nestled in the four walls of our homes and isolated from the very ones who are willing and able to make this mom journey with us. In Ruth and Naomi's day, families often lived on the same property and even in the same house. In many countries today that still is true.

When my husband, our youngest son and I lived in Costa Rica, we were often invited to a precious family's home. We affectionately called the patriarch of the home "Papa Juan." The matriarch was Momma Profidia. Situated in their home was a small dining area on the left just inside the door. On the right was an open doorway to the outdoor kitchen where a tin roof shielded the area from the rain. The hall seemed long for such a small home, but as we made our way to the end, we noticed there were no walls. Sheets separated the padded beds that lined the floor one after the other on both sides.

At any given time, 24 family members lived in that tiny 1,000-square-foot block home with concrete floors and a tin roof. It wasn't a decorating diva's idea of beautiful, but it was a beautiful thing, nonetheless. Most of the 24 lived under one roof in the main house. Others built small houses on a nearby plot of the family-owned land—just steps away from the ones they loved.

Papa Juan and Mama Profidia's home is one where traditions are passed down daily and young girls grow up knowing that the words "For better or worse; for richer or poorer; 'til death do us part" are much more than words recited from the lips of a beautiful young woman wearing a white wedding dress. They know because they live among married couples who are in the trenches of what marriage is all about, and they see them make it work through the good, the bad and the ugly. They are strengthened by other women in their family: women who walk through difficult times and come out on the other side stronger and even more dedicated to the God to whom they have surrendered and the husband to whom they are committed.

They know what it means to manage their homes well because their mommas did. They cook together, clean together, laugh and cry together. They even fuss and fight with one another. They do life together and all are better for it.

A young momma learns what a good mom is not only by watching those who have gone before her but also because they hold her hand along the way. She doesn't feel the total weight of every decision because other moms help her in times of need.

When her baby won't stop crying and she doesn't know what to do, those moms are there. When he throws a temper tantrum and she's at her wits end, they are there. When he goes through the terrible twos and the tumultuous threes, and she feels ready to scream, they are there.

Through thick and thin, through every season, they are there and each generation is better because the women who came before them are willing to walk through life with them.

A Different World

In the land of the free and the home of the brave, we don't live like that. We live in a different world. We don't commune as they did in the days of Ruth and Naomi, and we certainly don't dwell with 24 other family members in a 1,000-square-foot home. We don't ask for help because we've got it—we can do it ourselves. So we struggle and our families suffer because we pull into the driveway, enter our homes, close our doors and shut everyone else out. Life, however, isn't meant to be lived alone. We *can't* get it all done by ourselves and we *don't* have all the answers. We're human—we need each other, and that's okay.

Sweet mom, there are other mothers all around you. Some who are in your shoes, some who have walked the path of mommy-hood before you. They are the family, friends, coworkers and mentoring mommas whose lives teach us what it looks like to do this mom thing well. They form a community of mothers who stand ready to lend a listening ear and a helping hand.

They don't always get it right either. They aren't Pinterest-perfect moms who know how to make every meal from scratch and craft their way to an award-winning decor. But they can help you navigate the uncharted waters of parenting because they've set sail through those parental seas before.

You don't have to feel alone, inadequate or ill-equipped. Your 24/7 gig called motherhood is a joint journey, and there are women who are willing to walk with you along the way. In order to take one step of your journey with another mom, you will need to take the first step of the journey by intentionally meeting her.

Kim is surrounded by children all day long, yet she often feels very alone. Many moms feel the same way, but they don't have to—and neither do you. There is a resurgence of mentoring mammas who are ready and willing to step into their Titus 2 shoes and love you through your journey. Yes . . . mentoring. "Mentoring" may be an old-fashioned word, but in our modern day, there is great need for it. In fact, mentoring is not an archaic concept; it's just a dated word for community.

A Fresh Look at an Age-Old Word

Tragically lost in a generation that gravitates to innovative words and chic phrases, mentoring has not only lost its name, but also it has lost its place. But that is changing, and women are stepping into their mentoring shoes like never before. The online presence of mentoring ministries and Titus 2 websites is growing rapidly, and many churches are implementing mentoring ministries for the first time. Like an army of women linking hearts and hands to change the world, a new breed of women is taking on an old role to create a new culture of community. These are women who live next door and who you see at the malls and in grocery stores. You may find them sitting in churches and sensing that they are to make a difference in this world full of mothers who feel alone and lonely in their journeys as moms. They understand that the silence of the mothers of their generation has hurt those who are coming behind them, and they are standing together to become a community who helps others do motherhood well.

Dear mom, it is how we do life best. Together. It's happening all around us. Many of us see the need to not only be a mentor but to consistently be mentored as well. When you think about it, Titus 2 calls us to live on both sides of the mentoring equation: the mentor and the mentee. It's the way it is supposed to be. Every time you go to lunch with a friend and talk about what you are going through and she shares a word of wisdom, you have just been mentored. Every time you walk with a friend who is going through a difficult time and you encourage her heart, you have just mentored her.

We may be independent, but we don't have to remain isolated. We were created for community; but in our culture, living in community with one another has to be intentional if it is to be at all. Perhaps you feel alone somewhere between the crayon-colored walls, car pools, and the roll of toilet paper your little one just dropped into the toilet. Maybe you feel the world expects you to live life with a cape, a lasso, or a tiara on your head like some kind of Wonder Mom. But moms who have been there and done that know that the real "mom life" isn't easy. They know that moms are better together, and that *alone* is a very lonely place to be.

While your children are home, your window of influence and the opportunity to mold their hearts is wide open—but one day your nest will be empty and you will only be given limited access to speak truth and life into your children's lives. When they are young are the days when you want to make your impact as a mother count. Let someone who has been where you are listen to your heart as you maneuver your way through motherhood. Allow yourself the blessing of soaking in some words of wisdom from a mom who is willing to share her own fears, failures and successes.

Your precious children are looking to you to be a living example they can follow. They will do what you do and trust what you say. They will look up to their father and seek his approval, but you are the one who nurtures their heart through life. *You* are their primary mentor.

While ministering to moms, I've often quoted the following words uttered by Abraham Lincoln about his mother:

All that I am, or hope to be, I owe to my angel mother.

I couldn't help but wonder how Abraham Lincoln's mamma ended up being such a bright light in his life when she only had nine short years to spend with him. What wisdom did she glean at the feet of her own parents who were Quakers? Was she just a naturally inspiring mom or did a family member or friend leave deep imprints on her heart that made her the momma Abraham Lincoln admired so deeply? Perhaps someone planted seeds in her heart as she was growing up and someone else came along and fertilized those seeds while she was raising her child.

We don't really know, but we do know that her son, Abraham, echoed the heart of almost every child on the planet: "All that I am, or hope to be, I owe to my angel mother." For good or bad, our children learn from their mommas. Mothers mold the heart of the next generation. But to do it well, we need each other. We're not alone in this wide world of motherhood. We have each other. We just need to be willing to step outside our own lives to find each other.

Iron sharpens iron, so a friend sharpens a friend (Prov. 27:17, *NLT*).

A Prayer for Mom

Lord, I have to confess that being a mom is hard. I don't have all the answers and I don't want to try to do motherhood alone. I ask You not only to join me in this journey but I also ask You to lead the way. You tell us in Your Word that "two are better than one" (Eccles. 4:9), that "in a multitude of counselors there is safety" (Prov. 24:6), and that "iron sharpens iron" (Prov. 27:17). Please surround me with godly mothers who have been where I am and who will speak truth, encouragement and wisdom into my life so that I can be the best mom I can possibly be. Precious heavenly Father, please help me point my children to You, not only by what I say, but also by the way I parent my children and live my life.

More for Mom

A Familiar Look
1. Have you ever noticed that overwhelmed momma look on another mother?
2. How do you handle it when you feel overwhelmed?

Kim's Story
3. How can you relate to Kim's story of feeling alone?
4. Have you ever felt you and your children didn't live up to others' expectations?

Naomi and Ruth
5. When you read through the story of Naomi and Ruth, you can't help but wonder what it is that would make Ruth cling to Naomi. What is it in a friend that would make you stick with her through thick and thin?
6. What is it that you would look for in a mentor? And would you prefer her to be Pinterest perfect or would you be glad that she wasn't?

A Different World
7. Do you think our independence hinders our aptness to foster relationships with other women, and what can you do personally to assure that you enjoy the community of moms?

A Fresh Look at an Age-Old Word
8. Do you feel that mentoring is old-fashioned, or is it still important?
9. How could mentoring minister to your need now?

2

IT'S A BEAUTIFUL LIFE

You made all the delicate, inner parts of my body and knit me together in my mother's womb. Thank you for making me so wonderfully complex! Your workmanship is marvelous—how well I know it.
PSALM 139:13-14

How does a mom stay focused on God's plan and purpose for her precious little one when her days are filled with endless piles of laundry, dried spaghetti sauce in the carpet and temper tantrums in the produce section of the grocery store? Whether you are just beginning your journey through pregnancy or you are seeing your children off to school, this chapter, "It's a Beautiful Life," uses stories and biblical insight to help mothers consistently embrace the beautiful truth that each child is a masterpiece, carefully crafted by the Creator of the universe . . . a divine design . . . intentionally shaped by the heart of God—and so is she.

The Making of a Masterpiece

She was frightened by the way he tried to control her and she knew it was time to tell him that she didn't want to see him anymore. She agreed to go out with him one more time, but only because she felt it would be easier to break up that way.

As she began to tell him it was over, his response to her rejection erupted into rage and Faye was brutally raped. After it was over, she pretended everything was fine in the hope he wouldn't hurt her anymore. When he took her home, she shut the apartment door behind her, slid down the wall, curled up into a ball and wept for what seemed like a lifetime.

Faye tucked the terrible attack in her heart and didn't tell a soul. Like many who suffer such a horrific event, she was paralyzed with fear. As days turned into weeks, she felt like it was too late to go to the police, so she suffered in silence.

Just a little over a month after her attack, Faye was faced with yet another tragedy. She was pregnant and she knew the baby belonged to the man who had ruthlessly attacked her. That was 1962 and the baby she was carrying was me. I was the result of her tragic rape. Not just an unwanted pregnancy, but a woman's worst nightmare.

Emotions run deep for a woman who has walked through the unimaginable, but somehow my birth mom saw past the pain. With the choice of a back-alley abortion staring her in the face and the pressure from her peers to terminate the pregnancy, she knew that ending her pregnancy would not put an end to her pain—it would only intensify it.

Faye courageously confronted the coming months with the determination to do what was right in spite of what others said or what she had been through. Her heart rested in the fact that the baby she was carrying was a life like every other life, regardless of the way it was conceived.

But pregnancy is different for everyone. Whether pink lines, a plus sign or a doctor's diagnosis is the way you discover you are expecting, a multitude of thoughts and emotions are sure to follow. Some women are excited and receive the news with great anticipation. Others are afraid of what their future might hold and aren't sure how they are going to deal with the days ahead.

We've heard it said that life begins at conception, but is that true? When does life really begin? Perhaps we've had it all wrong. We think in terms of time and space. However, according to the Bible, life truly begins in the heart and mind of the Living God long before conception takes place.

The conditions of conception do not determine the value of a life. In our minds there may be accidental parents, but in the mind of God there are no accidental people. Each one is a masterpiece—each person is a miracle created by God in spite of the way that sweet baby was conceived.

> The child must know that he is a miracle, that since the beginning of the world there hasn't been, and until the end of the world there will not be another child like him.—Pablo Casals

Knowing What's Growing

Sometimes it's good to go back to basics . . . to consider the marvelous miracle of birth . . . to discover how the Creator of the Universe carefully crafts each precious child. So, let's get a glimpse at what goes on inside the womb—let's just take a minute to marvel at the work of our Maker.

As we walk through the wonder of the life within, be sure not to let the scientific lingo lessen the beauty of it all. It's an extraordinary thing to see how every single life is most definitely a Divine design!

Each day that tiny treasure is hidden securely in the womb, the mother is a vital part of the making of a miracle. That little one is developing at warp speed and, although a mother propably doesn't realize it, God is in the midst of making something magnificent within her womb.

Scientifically, the process goes something like this:

- After ovulation the egg that has been released into the fallopian tubes awaits fertilization. When one sperm cell penetrates a mature egg, it becomes a fertilized egg and instantly the sex of the baby is determined.
- From the time the chromosomes collide, fertilization takes place and a baby begins its journey in life.
- The fertilized egg is called a zygote and is only about the size of a grain of salt, yet the genetic makeup is already complete. That means the gender, hair color, eye color, height, weight, skin tone and even fingerprints of that baby have already been determined.

- The zygote immediately begins its journey through the fallopian tubes where it travels for about three or four days before it attaches itself (called implantation) to the wall of the womb. During this time, the placenta begins to form. The placenta is what nourishes the baby throughout the months of pregnancy.
- Within the first four weeks, the baby grows like crazy. The brain, heart, lungs, eyes, inner ears, mouth and digestive system begin to develop.
- The way a baby grows in the womb is a beautifully complicated process that reminds us of how great our God is. Think about it! This amazingly tiny life tucked in a mother's tummy is a Divine design—carefully crafted by the Creator of the Universe!

Doctors refer to this precious cargo as an "embryo" from the moment of conception to the eighth week of pregnancy. From the eighth week until birth the baby is called a "fetus." To God, that tiny treasure is His masterpiece.

For you formed my inward parts; you knitted me together in my mother's womb. I praise you, for I am fearfully and wonderfully made. Wonderful are your works; my soul knows it very well (Ps. 139:13-14, *ESV*).

During pregnancy, there is a host of wondrous happenings that take place in the womb as a baby develops. It can be a little scary, but God has a plan for that little life within and the momma is an intricate part of if all!

God's plan and purpose for your child isn't affected by the way your baby was conceived. His desire for you and your little one isn't derailed by your circumstances. Each child began his or her journey in the heart of God long before time began, not just to exist on this planet, but to live a life of purpose. The same is true for you, sweet momma! Jeremiah 29:11 tells us:

For I know the plans I have for you, declares the Lord, plans for welfare and not for evil, to give you a future and a hope (*ESV*).

Heather's Story

Heather was just a teenager when she became pregnant with her first child. After a routine ultrasound, the nurse came in with a frown on her face. Heather may have been young, but she knew trouble when she saw it. Her boyfriend squeezed her hand as the nurse asked her to sit down. "We are scheduling you for an amniocentesis. The test results indicate your child has Down Syndrome. It's not worth continuing the pregnancy and it's best for you to terminate," the nurse said as she scribbled on her chart.

"Abortion? No, I couldn't do that!" Tons of emotions erupted in Heather's heart but she resolved to keep her baby no matter what. It didn't matter if the baby would be born with a disability, nor did it matter if her boyfriend chose to stay with her or not. She didn't even care that family and friends were advising her to terminate her pregnancy. An abortion was out of the question!

Thirteen years have passed and Heather is still thankful she chose life. Her boyfriend became her husband and Heather says that although their daughter, Cheyenne, has Asperger's, she is the biggest joy of her life. Heather thinks Cheyenne is perfect just the way she is. It hasn't been an easy road, but Heather insists, "With my husband and God on my side, it has been the greatest journey."

The value of life isn't found in how healthy or "perfect" the life is. It is found in the fact that every person on the planet is fearfully and wonderfully made by God and He has a plan and a purpose for each life.

I may have been the result of a horrific rape, but when, at the age of 27, I met my birth mom, I noticed she never talked about how painful it was to carry me for nine months. She only reflected on how hard it was to place me in another woman's arms and say goodbye for what might have been forever.

To others, I may have been a product of rape—something to be discarded. To God, I was His creation and He had a plan for my life. I'm so thankful my birth mom realized that.

Divine Design

In Psalm 139, David describes God's lavish love for His creation. I *love* the words David used . . . knit together . . . a wonderfully

complex and marvelous workmanship intricately woven together by the Living God. That's the beauty of the mystery of
life. David knew he was a Divine design, and so were you, and
so was your sweet little child.

Don't you love knowing that we did not just ooze from a
jillion-year-old slime pit or somehow morph from a monkey into
a man? We were created by God—and we were created for God.

Recently, I was doing a little digging in Scripture and I came
across a sweet nugget of truth that I think will make your heart
smile big time. Look at how just one word clearly communicates
the miracle of life.

In Genesis 1:1 (*ESV*) we find these words: "In the beginning
God created the heaven and the earth." And in Genesis 1:27
(*ESV*), the Bible says, "God created man in His own image, in the
image of God He created him; male and female He created them."

The very first verb we come across in the Bible is the word
"created." Because the English language does not convey the
complete essence of this word, we can't really fathom its magnitude. (Hang with me for a minute, because I think this will blow
your mind! I know it did mine.)

The original word for "created" (see Gen. 1:1) is the Hebrew
word *bará*. It means exactly what you think it does: to create,
form, shape or fashion. But the beautiful surprise is that in the
40-plus times this specific form of the word "create" is found
in Scripture, it is not combined with any other subject but
God. If grammar isn't your thing, let me help you see it a bit
more clearly. God (subject) created (verb) man (direct object).
Whenever you find the word *bará* (created), God is the One doing
the creating.

Think about that! God's choice of words leaves us no room
to doubt the nature of our existence. Only God can *bará* (create). There is no mistake about it—He is our Creator! He is *the*
Creator! Don't you just love how God makes Himself known
to us in ways we have yet to discover?! (Oh, please tell me that
rocks your world like it does mine!) You're someone special,
sweet mom! And so is that sweet little baby of yours!

Jeremiah the prophet thought he was special too. Look at
how he described God's plan and purpose in his own conception:

Before I formed you in the womb I knew you, before you were born I set you apart; I appointed you as a prophet to the nations (Jer. 1:5, *NIV*).

Jeremiah was etched on the heart of God long before he breathed his first breath. God's purpose for him was defined before he was even able to understand what a prophet was.

Sweet mom, you were in God's heart before you ever entered your mother's womb. The same is true for your baby. The process of pregnancy is nothing short of the making of a miracle—a miracle that includes you.

Defining "Mom"

I was only 17 and, though young in years, I was more mature than I should have been. A decade of sexual abuse has a way of erasing innocence and adding years at the same time. My skewed view of love led me down a road I wasn't ready for and I found myself standing in the bathroom staring at the positive results of a home pregnancy test and wondering what in the world I was going to do.

I was a girl with a bad past and a bleak future with a baby on the way and I was scared. I had no idea what a mother is or what a mother does, yet for some reason it never crossed my mind that it was time to get some much-needed guidance. At 17, I wasn't wise enough to know that I needed wisdom for the lifelong journey ahead.

Becoming a mom was something I thought would come naturally, and in some ways it did. But I didn't really grasp the gravity of it all. I remember my entry into motherhood was something like the crash landing a meteor makes when it's hurled from space and plows into a planet. Random. With no direction and no destination. I wasn't sure about what I was supposed to be doing, but I knew I loved being a mom.

As I look in the rearview mirror of my mom journey, I can't help but wonder what I was thinking. Why did I think that just because I had a mom, I knew how to be one? Seriously! I had a family doctor but it didn't mean I was ready to pick up a scalpel and perform surgery. I had a dentist but it didn't mean I was ready to fill a cavity. I even had a teacher but it didn't mean I knew how to be one.

If I had wanted to become a doctor, dentist or teacher I would have needed some kind of training; and while each of those positions is not only highly noble but also very significant, there is no more important role than that of a mother. Being a mom is a 24/7 lifelong gig that molds the hearts and lives of the next generation. It's the most important job on the planet and it comes with the most beautiful title in the world—the title of "Mom."

Typically, a mom has a baby and begins doing whatever comes next. Sometimes she seeks advice or digs deep looking for the how-tos of raising children. But what if a mom decided to discover what her new role in life entailed long before, or even soon after, the baby was born? Do you think defining motherhood would change the way she does mom?

Sleepless nights and overflowing mounds of spit-up-laden baby clothes kept me moving forward into motherhood, but doing the next thing and the next thing and the next only kept me busy. It didn't make me a better mom nor did it help me understand how important it is to parent with a plan and a purpose.

I remember a trip I made to New Orleans when I was only 22. I didn't have a map and it was about 15 years before the invention of the GPS. So, basically, I had to wing it. I had never traveled that way before so I wasn't sure where I was going. It was unfamiliar territory and after far too many wrong turns, a lot of wasted time and many missed stops along the way, I finally arrived at my intended destination.

I got where I wanted to go, but I made a lot of mistakes along the way. The journey was more difficult than it should have been, and if I had been wise, I would have sought the advice of someone who had traveled that road before.

Being a mom without a plan or purpose is kind of like taking a trip and not knowing where you're going. That's why defining what a mother is, and what a mother does, is foundational to your own journey as a mom. It's like placing stones on the path that lies before you so that you know which steps to take and why. Whether your children are infants or teenagers, it's not too late to start paving the way to purposeful parenting.

The unknown journey we moms take into motherhood is also the best reason on the planet to find a mentoring momma who has navigated the bumpy roads past the baby bump. Being a mom is not always easy and the road is not normally smooth. A mentor can help bring clarity to the journey ahead and help you foresee what she has already seen along the way. You may not think a mentor is necessary, but when it comes to knowing where the parenting potholes are, which roads a mom should avoid, and how to discover your coveted destination, a mentor is better than any GPS could ever be.

So, what is a mom? According to TheFreeDictionary.com, a mom is "a woman who becomes pregnant and gives birth to a child, adopts a child or raises a child." How can such a simple definition define such a powerful three-letter word: "mom"? I don't know who came up with that definition, but if you've been a mom for more than a day you know that a mother is much more than a female parent. A mom is a woman who molds lives and holds the heart of the next generation in her hands, and her identity is intrinsically linked with what she does.

Moms are multitasking mavens who wear a multitude of hats. They are Wonder Women of sorts. They may not sport a golden lasso or be clothed with a cape, but they are definitely women who juggle life in superhero-like fashion and change the world every day.

Moms Are . . .
Cooks, counselors, confidants and chauffeurs.

They are event planners, menu planners, errand runners
and bookkeepers.

Moms are nurturers, nurses, coaches and
cake decorators.

They mop, they shop, they teach and they preach.

They organize homes, maximize opportunities,
minimize stress and synchronize events.

Moms clean toilets, dishes, laundry and sticky fingers.

They establish the atmosphere in the home with
just a word or even a tone.

Moms work hard, sleep little, laugh a lot and cry often.

They encourage, discourage, discipline and train.

Moms are a shoulder to cry on, a heart that listens
and a hand that upholds.

Moms mold lives and help determine destinies.

But the most important thing a mother does . . . *she loves.*

Perhaps you read through that partial Wonder Woman list
and wonder how in the world a mom does it all. Maybe you realize that list describes your life and you are wondering how *you*
do it all. I'm not sure where you are in your journey, but I know
God has a great plan for your life and that plan includes the most
important role on the planet—the role of Mom. A mom is defined
not by simply being a female parent, but by what she does every
day—that's what makes a mom.

Defining your identity as a mom does more than validate your
role in life; it gives you a vision for the life you are molding and
prepares you to be a parent with a plan and a purpose—a mom
who is defined not only by who she is but also by what she does.
It's like having a roadmap for motherhood.

Tucked in the tummy of every expectant mother is a little life
that depends on her to understand the magnitude of each moment of motherhood. So whether you are carrying your baby in
your womb, in your arms or picking that sweet little one up from
school, your precious child is God's masterpiece.

God creates those tiny treasures we call children, but He uses
mothers to paint strokes of love, character and integrity into their
hearts and lives. You are the brush, sweet mom, and you only get
one chance to choose each stroke well.

It's the heart of a mom who is able to look past the poopy diapers, runny noses and chocolate milk smeared on her new white blouse to see the miracle God has given her—the one who depends on her to be his/her biggest cheerleader, most reliable example and most dedicated prayer warrior.

It's a beautiful life, sweet mom, and the Lord has intentionally picked you to be a critical part of it all. Amazing, huh?

A Prayer for Mom

Lord, I love knowing You are our Creator and that Your Word says we are fearfully and wonderfully made (see Ps. 139:13-14)! The complexity of Your creation is intoxicating! It's beyond my capacity to comprehend, yet it keeps me longing for a deeper, more intimate knowledge of You and a passionate appreciation for Your great love for me and my children. Father, please help me never forget that You have a plan and a purpose for us, especially in the middle of the messiness of motherhood. It's really such a beautiful life—this life You have given us. Help me to always treasure the truth that You treasure each of us!

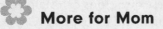 **More for Mom**

The Making of a Masterpiece
1. Take a moment to reflect on the day you found out you were pregnant and describe the various emotions you experienced and why.

Knowing What's Growing
2. Does knowing a bit about the miracle that takes place within the womb cause you to consider your purpose as a mom or your child's purpose in life any differently?

Heather's Story
3. Can you relate to Heather's story in any way?
4. How can pressure from other people cause you to do something you would regret?

Divine Design

5. Genesis 1:27 says, "So God created man in His own image; in the image of God He created him; male and female He created them." How does knowing that we are created by God make a difference in what we think about parenting?
6. Have you ever thought about yourself as a masterpiece that was carefully crafted by the Creator of the universe?
7. How does knowing you are a masterpiece help you understand your value and the value of your precious child?
8. Read through Psalm 139:13-18 and describe how it makes you feel to know that you and your little one were carefully crafted by the Creator of the universe?

Defining "Mom"

9. How do you think it can change the process of parenting if you have a plan and a purpose?
10. How would you define yourself as a mom and how is who you are intrinsically linked to what you do?
11. Below is a list of 10 questions to ask yourself as you pull back the covers of your morning and start your mom journey for the day. Read through them and then consider how asking yourself these questions can help you parent more effectively with a plan and a purpose.

Parenting with a **Plan** and a **Purpose**

1. How can I parent my children today in a way that will point them to a relationship with Jesus Christ?
2. What character traits can I work on developing in my children today?
3. What struggles are they having that I can help them learn to overcome?
4. What can I do to help them see the need to care for others?
5. How can I teach them to serve their family and their community?
6. How can I teach them to submit to authority today?

7. What have I done today to instill a deep prayer life in my children?
8. What bad habits or character flaws do I need to help them deal with today?
9. What do I want them to ultimately learn as a result of the circumstances they are in?
10. What example do I demonstrate to them that will strengthen their resolve to become men and women of God?

3

A DIFFERENT ME

For everything there is a season, a time for every activity under heaven.
ECCLESIASTES 3:1, *NLT*

The moment a baby is conceived, a mother is also born and everything changes. Whether she is a young teen mom who is struggling to step into her new identity or a corporate business woman trying to juggle her new life as a mom, "A Different Me" incorporates real-life stories that will help mothers understand why life as they once knew it has been forever altered.

"A Different Me" will also provide them with the necessary tools to deal with the emotions and questions that are sure to follow.

Losing Myself

Time seemed to stand still as I gazed into his hazy eyes and he wrapped his tiny fingers around mine. I wasn't prepared for how mesmerized I would be the moment I saw his face and held his soft little body in my arms. But there he was, my newborn son, brand new to the big wide world around him. I felt as if I had loved him my whole life.

I was barely 18 years old and the thought of having a baby made my heart smile. Finally, someone I could love who would love me back. After living through a decade of sexual abuse as a child, my heart yearned for an untainted love and a life of significance. And, somehow, I thought having a child would provide that.

I couldn't imagine anything sweeter than a lifetime of cuddling my baby boy. But real life doesn't play out in freeze-frame fashion. Everything changes. I just didn't realize how much change was in store for me.

It didn't take long for me to discover that being a mom comes with sleepless nights, nonstop days and more work than I had ever imagined. I loved being a mom, but the visions of motherhood that danced in my head long before my son was born did not match my everyday reality.

As far back as I can remember, I had always wanted to be a wife and mother; but a wife and a mother wasn't all I wanted to be. I had dreams of being a nurse or a teacher or perhaps even an archaeologist. But life doesn't always turn out as we plan. The choices we make sometimes derail our dreams and leave us wondering what coulda, woulda and shoulda been.

I didn't realize it at the time, but becoming pregnant in high school can kind of put a kink in the best of plans. And that's exactly what happened to me: pregnant at 17, married and divorced by 19.

When you are a single mom trying to do all and be all, it's pretty tough to think beyond the diapers and the unpaid bills. Your new idea of success means putting food on the table and a roof over your heads.

The years passed and marriage once again loomed over my life. I was soon remarried and had another baby on the way and I was becoming what I always wanted to be, a wife and a mother. But sometimes I wondered, *Is that all there is?* Did the words "wife" and "mother" completely define my existence? And what about the future? When my children grow up and my days are no longer filled with dirty diapers, field trips and homeschool? What will I do with my time?

I had always believed that being a mother was the greatest calling on the planet. As women, it is our opportunity to mold the heart of the next generation and leave a legacy of faith. But I knew the day was coming when my home would no longer be filled with a flurry of teenagers traipsing in and out of the house. I realized the day was fast approaching when those sweet, nighttime prayers by the bedside and those daily doses of butterfly kisses would end. What then? Had I completely lost who I was supposed to be by becoming who I was?

Unsure about what was ahead, I turned to God's Word where I found just the right amount of light for the next step. Proverbs 16:9 (*KJV*) says, "A man's heart plans his way, but the LORD directs his steps." And in Psalm 37:23 (*KJV*), we find, "The steps of a good man are ordered by the LORD, and He delights in his way."

My heart's desire to become a wife and a mother was fulfilled. I wasn't a Christian when my children were born, but I became one soon after the birth of my second son. As I look back on the way my life has changed over the years, I'm reminded of how God graciously made all things work together for good according to His promise in Romans 8:28—even that which happened before I knew Him. He also placed a desire in my heart to minister to moms. All moms. And so here I am, writing this book to encourage you in your mom journey.

God has given me the amazing privilege of ministering to women in whatever season of life they may find themselves. He has helped me encourage broken lives and hurting hearts with the unchanging, life-changing Word of God. I didn't lose myself when I became a wife and a mother; I just stepped into the person He created me to be. I may have taken some detours and wandered off the beaten path, but the Lord has used each step of my way to help me become who I was created to be.

Through the years, I've had to release a few dreams along the way, but when I look in the rearview mirror of my life, I can see that if those dreams had come true, my life would not be what it is. Those dreams might have turned out to be nightmares instead.

Who we are today may not look anything like who we thought we would be when we were young and life seemed so much simpler. However, if we surrender our lives to Christ and seek to do His will, He will direct our steps and define our lives so much better than our teen dreams possibly could have.

He alone makes beauty out of the ashes of our past and brings healing and hope to our hurting hearts. He alone knows what our next step should be. And when we follow Him, we won't lose ourselves—we will find ourselves. He will help us discover that all the changes that occur when we become mothers will be the stuff that makes us stronger and yet more dependent than ever on God.

Those things we feel we had to give up, those dreams we may feel we had to release, and those changes we had to make in our lives pale in comparison to our biggest blessings. And what are they? They are the ones who call us "Mom."

How Motherhood Changed Mary

Although we can't be sure, tradition and theologians tell us that Mary was somewhere between the age of 13 and 16 when she gave birth to Jesus. Young in age but wise beyond her years, her surprise pregnancy was destined to change her life.

In a day when virginity was valued, marriage was sacred, and cultural traditions were held dear, Mary found herself with child before she had a sexual encounter with a man. A miracle from God, yes, but this miracle left her with a whole lot of explaining to do in an era when adultery was punishable by death.

> Now the birth of Jesus Christ took place in this way. When his mother Mary had been betrothed to Joseph, before they came together she was found to be with child from the Holy Spirit. And her husband Joseph, being a just man and unwilling to put her to shame, resolved to divorce her quietly. But as he considered these things, behold, an angel of the Lord appeared to him in a dream, saying, "Joseph, son of David, do not fear to take Mary as your wife, for that which is conceived in her is from the Holy Spirit. She will bear a son, and you shall call his name Jesus, for he will save his people from their sins." All this took place to fulfill what the Lord had spoken by the prophet: "Behold, the virgin shall conceive and bear a son, and they shall call his name Immanuel" (which means, God with us). When Joseph woke from sleep, he did as the angel of the Lord commanded him: he took his wife, but knew her not until she had given birth to a son. And he called his name Jesus (Matt. 1:18-25, *ESV*).

God had gifted Mary and her man with an angelic message of her miraculous conception. They may have trusted that God had chosen their journey for them, but they were still in for a bumpy ride.

Sometimes we read though the Bible and gloss over each page as if the people weren't real and their circumstances didn't rock their world as ours do us. Bible people were real people, with real fears and real feelings, just like those you and I have.

Joseph was a righteous man and chose to shelter Mary from shame; but how does a man deal with the overwhelming reality that his betrothed is pregnant and that he is not the father, and then the discovery that she has been divinely selected to carry and raise the Savior of the world?

How does a young woman, who was most likely still a teenager, deal with an unexpected pregnancy? How could she face a rough ride on the back of a donkey within days of her delivery date? What went through her mind when her husband had to make a frantic but unsuccessful late-night search for a hotel room? How did she feel when her weary and worn-out pregnant body lay down at night only to discover she was in labor? What was she thinking when she had a nighttime delivery in a dirty stable surrounded by the smell of animals? What emotions did she experience when she gave birth to her long-awaited baby boy yet had no place to lay him except for a filthy feeding trough? How's that for an *overwhelming* introduction to motherhood?

Mary's life went from one extreme to another overnight. She was a carefree teen with dreams that most likely didn't even come close to being chosen by God to carry the long-awaited Savior. God had plans for her life—plans that were better than anything she could have dreamed of on her own. Plans that would require strength, courage, faith and sacrifice.

Mary bravely charted a course for motherhood, but her parenting years were marked with a multitude of mountain-sized hurdles and faith-trying challenges. She wasn't just an obscure woman with a fictional life. She was just like you and me. Oh, we may not be chosen to carry the Savior of the world, but we have been chosen to carry someone who, we pray, will proclaim Him. Mary was a woman whose life was changed by motherhood. And so are you and I.

Linda's Story

Linda was a 35-year-old career woman when she married the love of her life. With a looming health issue that would potentially make it difficult to have children, and with her biological clock ticking, she and her husband decided to try to have children as soon as possible.

Linda had a plan. She expected it to take about two years for her to conceive. In the meantime, she could continue to concentrate on her career as an assistant marketing director for a large talk radio station in California. She was an established career woman who had worked hard to get where she was, and she loved what she did. Her schedule was filled with corporate meetings, marketing campaigns, events planning and program deadlines. She had to be available 24/7 and at a moments notice, but she didn't mind that her dream job was so demanding. She was used to making plans and scheduling her life.

Her two-year pregnancy plan didn't work out the way she expected it to.

The first month the couple tried to get pregnant, they did, and from that moment forward everything changed. Linda was a woman who thrived in a corporate environment with the pressures of deadlines and details, but suddenly she was a new wife with a baby on the way.

When her little bundle of joy arrived on the scene, her maternal heart began to wrestle with her new identity. During her four-month maternity leave, she started searching for the perfect childcare for her baby girl. After signing up to be on the waiting list for the best possible daycare she could find, she received a call that there was an opening.

It was a great daycare. It had a wonderful reputation and they did a jam-up job taking care of the children in their care. There was nothing really wrong with the daycare, but something started tugging at Linda's heart. She started asking herself questions such as, "What if my baby cries and they are busy with other children?" "What if she gets sick and they can't take the time to comfort her?" "Why am I leaving my baby in a daycare anyway?"

Then it happened. The proverbial straw that broke the maternal camel's back. Linda walked in the door of the daycare and one of the workers asked her to leave three days of clothing and supplies in the event there was an earthquake or other emergency and she wasn't able to get to the daycare to pick up her daughter. Suddenly her dream job paled in comparison to her darling little daughter. Linda decided it was time to make some changes. She and her hubby started discussing the possibility of Linda staying home. On paper, they couldn't swing it financially, but she still felt it was what the Lord wanted her to do. Linda turned in her corporate clothes for jeans and a T-shirt, and instead of racing from board rooms to business meetings, Linda now rushes from playgrounds to play dates.

Having children changes everything. Linda's life morphed from all things business to all things baby. Her world is completely different, but she wouldn't change it for the world.

Heather's Story

Heather's story is much like mine, yet very different. With an over-whelmed heart and tears running down her cheeks, she called her aunt and asked, "Can you come pick me up for a day or two?" Her precious new bundle of joy, Cheyenne, was throwing another unexplained crying fit and she didn't have a clue what to do. After she hung up the phone, she began to reflect on how she had dreamed her life would be—and this was definitely not it.

Heather's new reality as a mother was more than she could handle, and the monumental demands of motherhood were finally catching up with her. Within five months, she had graduated high school, moved out of her mom's home, moved in with her boyfriend, got married and gave birth. Somehow, she thought being married to her boyfriend and facing the world together would make life easy. Instead, she was alone up to 12 hours a day while her husband, Chris, went to school and worked two jobs to support them.

Heather was in a new city, without a vehicle, without a friend and without a clue. Baby Cheyenne needed her all the time and since none of her friends wanted to make the two-hour trip to visit her, she felt completely and utterly alone.

Gone were the days of carefree living, picking up at a moment's notice, cheering for the football team and shopping at the mall with friends. Instead, Heather's life was now filled with sleepless nights, dirty diapers, sore breasts and learning to navigate the tumultuous waters of a new marriage.

Heather is in her thirties now, a mother of three and still married to her high school sweetheart. Through the years, she has discovered what it takes to be the mother her children need her to be. With years of marriage and mothering under her belt, she not only understands the umpteen transitions that take place over time, but she also knows that when it is all said and done, being a mom is the best job on the planet.

A Brand New Point of View

It wasn't something I expected to happen. It wasn't even on my radar. But wow! How my perspective changed the moment my baby boy was born!

I thought pregnancy had prepared me for the way I would think after I gave birth to my firstborn son, but I had no idea that the gear-shifting that was going on in my heart would continue to create a new sense of parental protectiveness that I knew nothing about. Being a mom sure changes everything.

Recently, I talked to a single mom who has three little girls, and one of her biggest concerns was that she would be able to provide for her children, not only financially, but that they would receive the emotional support they needed. She was an overwhelmed momma who was trying to fill too many shoes and wear too many hats. She found it a challenge to pay the rent each month and put the next meal on the table.

Before she had her daughters, she wanted to be a career woman who had children later in life. After she had her first little girl, everything changed and her career was placed on the back burner and exchanged for baby food, diapers and a cute, cuddly, very dependent and needy newborn.

Another young mom savored the spontaneity of life as a teen and an early 20-something. Her life revolved around the next big event, and at the drop of a hat she was ready to head out the door and enjoy some fun with her friends.

When motherhood knocked on her door, everything changed. During her first two trimesters of pregnancy, she wondered how she was going to juggle life in the fast lane. When she hit her third trimester, her body put on the brakes for her. At first, she was pretty peeved. If she had to slow down at this point, what would it be like after her baby was born? Once she laid eyes on that brown-eyed boy, she really didn't care. Her perspective shifted as quickly as her priorities, and hanging out at the house with her baby in one arm and her hubby on the other became her new norm—and she loved every minute of it.

Funny how what once seemed so important becomes so insignificant in light of what really matters most once that sweet little baby is born! Being a mom might change everything, but there is no greater calling on the planet. This is our chance to mold the hearts of our children and the next generation. It's so easy to be overwhelmed by the loud cries of a cranky toddler and the relentless weight of responsibilities, but our call to motherhood is worth it all.

If you're new to the mom life, the following list of the changes that take place when you have a baby may be a fresh reality for you. If you've been a mom for a while, as you read through the list, I can almost hear you saying, "Amen, Sistah!"

Here's your "How Babies Change Everything" list:

1. Sleeping all night and sleeping in become occasional luxuries.
2. Your time is no longer your own.
3. You carry the responsibility to mold the heart of another human being.
4. You are now responsible to care for another life and put his or her needs before your own.
5. You live your life by your children's calendar with doctor appointments, play days, school schedules, church plays, sports, dance, art and music classes.
6. All of the sacrifices you have to make no longer seem like sacrifices.
7. You'd rather buy your child a new outfit or a toy than buy a new dress for yourself.
8. You'd rather give the last piece of cake to your child than eat it yourself because seeing his sweet smile makes your heart smile big time.
9. You have a whole new perspective on life, love and motherhood.

10. You find your inner momma bear when your children are threatened.
11. You wish you could pee in peace, but worry if the kids aren't sticking their fingers under the door.
12. You no longer put your needs and desires first.
13. You find that bodily functions are no longer gross because you get excited when your baby goes poo and when you are able to get a big boogie out of his nose.
14. You don't mind staying home every night because you understand your children will be grown before you know it and you will have all the time in the world to do things then.
15. You no longer watch real people on television. Instead your TV time is filled with puppets, people with costumes and all things animated.
16. You long for adult conversation but miss hearing "Mama" and "Dada" when you are away.
17. Your priorities change and you no longer think climbing the corporate ladder is the best thing you can do.
18. Slobbery kisses are sweet instead of gross.

Whether you are expecting your first bundle of joy or are a mom of three, the life you lived BK (before kids) was your own. Children have a way of changing all of that. But those little life-changing, thumb-sucking, bib-wearing babies are precious gifts from God.

Children are a heritage from the LORD, offspring a reward from him (Ps. 127:3, *NIV*).

Having children may rock your world and change your life, but they are a reward given to you by God. He sees every sacrifice you make, every sleepless night you go through, every time you rush to the emergency room, every event you have to miss because your children have somewhere to go, every time you find yourself cleaning throw-up off the bathroom floor or trying to scrub dried baby food off the carpet in your living room. Every time you have to sacrifice for your children, He sees it. He sees you.

You may change when you become a mom, but isn't that how it's supposed to be? What if you never changed? What would you be like at 30, 40 or 50 if you remained the same spontaneous and semi-responsible teen you once were? So, yes, being a mom changes everything—but as Rafiki said to Simba in *The Lion King*, "Change is good."

Yet God has made everything beautiful for its own time (Eccles. 3:11, *NLT*).

A Prayer for Mom

Lord, being a mom really does change everything! Please help me walk well as the new me. Help me understand the significance of this journey I am on and how everything I do and say affects my children in profound ways. Help me not look at the limits on my time as limitations to my life. Enable me to embrace my mom journey and all the changes that are ahead with joy, knowing that You know me, You see me, and You love me . . . and that You know, see and love my little ones too.

More for Mom

Losing Myself

1. What are the dreams you had when you were young about what you would do or be when you were older?
2. Was becoming a mother what you expected it would be? And how did it change your plans for your future?

How Motherhood Changed Mary

3. What are some things Mary had to face when she discovered she was pregnant?
4. I know it's speculation, but how do you think her pregnancy changed what she had in mind for her future?
5. Describe some ways that God's plan for her to have Jesus was far greater than anything she could have planned for herself.

Linda's Story

6. Linda's career was put on hold after she had her baby. What kind of emotional challenges might Linda have had to deal

with as a result of making the choice to stay home with her baby?

7. What are some challenges you are facing right now as a mother (or mother-to-be)?

Heather's Story

8. One of Heather's struggles was not having any friends with her on her mom journey. How can friends help you as a mom?

9. Heather is older now and the years have taught her so much more about being the kind of mother her children need. What are some things you think an older mother might understand that a younger mother doesn't?

A Brand New Point of View

10. How have your point of view and priorities changed since you became a mom?

11. Has the change been difficult for you, and if so, why?

12. Ecclesiastes 3:1 tells us there is a season for everything. How does that truth help you in your role as a mother?

4

HOW DO I LOVE THEE?

Love never fails.
1 Corinthians 13:8

How do I love thee? Let me count the ways.
I love thee to the depth and breadth and height My soul
can reach . . .
—Elizabeth Barrett Browning

These words may have dripped from the pen of Elizabeth Barrett Browning's lovesick heart, but counting the ways a mother loves her children is as endless as Elizabeth's love for her man. How do we love our children? What does love look like when it's more than words on a page? What does love really mean?

So often we attempt to love our children without really understanding what love actually means. In "How Do I Love Thee?" we will explore the concept of love and learn what it does and does not mean to love our children.

Love Is . . .

We talk about it. We sing about it. We're all looking for it. But do we really know what love is?

We typically filter our view of love through the lens of the way others have loved us. Unfortunately, that can give us a skewed view of what love really is. My own experience of childhood abuse left me with a distorted perspective of love. If we are going to love well, then we must first have a clear understanding of love.

Love isn't easy to define because it's subjective, elusive and ever-evolving. I love my husband, but I also love ice cream. I love my mom, but not the same way I love my husband and not the same way I love my friends, and definitely not the same way I love ice cream. Who, what and how I love have changed significantly between the ages of 14 and 40. The definition of love doesn't change, but my perception of it does.

When we look up the word "love" in a dictionary, we find that it means "deep affection" or "romantic attraction." But love is so much more than a four-letter word with a two-word definition.

So what is love? And what does it mean to really love our children? Take a minute and consider your own concept of love and then jot it down. You'll be surprised how much your view of love changes after we pull back the curtain and get a glimpse of what it really means.

A Mother's Love

I always thought that a mother's love for her child was something that came as naturally as breathing—as if love is a uniquely intrinsic part of a mother's heart. But Titus 2:4 tells us we have a whole lot of learning to do when it comes to loving our children:

> Older women likewise are to be reverent in their behavior, not malicious gossips nor enslaved to much wine, teaching what is good, so that they may encourage the young women to love their husbands, *to love their children* (Titus 2:3-4, *NASB*, emphasis added).

Older mothers are to mentor younger mothers and teach them to love their children. What? Really? I already love my children. It's funny how the years have a way of teaching us that love is greater than anything we ever imagined—so much more intentional than we might have ever considered.

Simply stated, love is doing what is best for the one who is loved. But the Bible tells us that God is love; therefore, it is only logical that we should derive our understanding of love from the One who defines it by His very existence. The Bible defines love in what is affectionately called "The Love Chapter": 1 Corinthians 13. This powerful passage of Scripture is something like a love test. It is a great filter through which moms can sift their actions and reactions and discover whether they are truly loving well.

LOVE—Biblically defined. Practically expressed:

- Love is patient—Love isn't easily angered: Patience is active endurance of opposition, long-suffering, steadfastness.[1] It is not giving up or giving in. A determination to do what is best for the one who is loved.
- Love is kind. It is not rude: "Kindness" is translated—gracious, virtuous, generous, gentleness, uprightness and goodness.[2] The opposite of harsh, hard, sharp or bitter.

A few weeks ago I was at a local store when I witnessed a young mom pushing her cart with one hand and holding a cell phone in her other hand. Her mind was on everything but her little toddler, who was scuffling along as fast as she could to keep up with her preoccupied momma.

"Mommy! Mommy! Mooommmmy!" she cried out, but her mom was too busy to listen. Again, I heard her blurt out, "Mommy!" Finally, she got her mother's attention. But instead of trying to find out what her precious child wanted, the mother turned around and shouted obscenities that should never be said at all—especially to a tender little tot.

She was neither patient nor kind. She was cruel and unloving. Regardless of whether that mom was suffering from extreme PMS or just distracted and disengaged by a phone call, that precious child will wear wounds on her heart that ointment and Band-Aids will never heal. Perhaps that momma never experienced kindness from her own parents. Kindness doesn't come easily for those who have experienced the opposite. If your past has been plagued with hard hearts and bitter words, you can still circumvent the cycle and create a home where kindness rules and rudeness is unacceptable.

- Love is not jealous: Does not envy, covet or jealously desire what it does not possess. Jealousy may be atypical of most mothers, but many women unconsciously covet the attention their babies get.
- Love does not covet what others have, especially when that someone is our children. Sweet mom, your children need you to be their greatest cheerleader and biggest fan. The world will be hard on their hearts and your applause will help them believe in themselves because you do.
- Love does not boast—is not proud—is not self-seeking. Love is not arrogant. It's selfless, not selfish. Love is all about the welfare of the one who is loved, not the recognition of the one who is supposed to be showing it.
- Love trusts—Trusting your children doesn't mean you are blind to their flaws and failures. Kids sometimes lie when they are caught with their hands in the proverbial cookie jar. They are masters at manipulation. But it is important that they know you trust them and that you set the example of honesty.
- Love hopes—Looking for the good in your child is paramount to nourishing a healthy self-esteem. A mom is the one person who sees the best in her child and holds out hope when all hope is gone. A mother loves with ceaseless hope.
- Love perseveres, never fails. No one on the planet can replace you. Your role as mom remains a constant source of dependable and undaunted love. You never stop being a mom, so you never stop loving your children.

A little biblical unveiling of what love is will cause us all to question if we really love those we say we do. If you want to know if you are loving your children well, give yourself the love test. Ask yourself:

- Was I just patient and kind?
- Did my response demonstrate jealousy, arrogance or pride?
- Was I rude, selfish or easily angered?
- Did I remind my child of everything she/he has ever done wrong?
- Did I rejoice in the truth?

- Did I protect, trust, hope and persevere in the way I responded to my child?

Love is patient, love is kind. It does not envy, it does not boast, it is not proud. It does not dishonor others, it is not self-seeking, it is not easily angered, it keeps no record of wrongs. Love does not delight in evil but rejoices with the truth. It always protects, always trusts, always hopes, always perseveres. Love never fails (1 Cor. 13:4-8, *NIV*).

An Inconvenient Love

When my children were babies, it seemed that every minute was filled with caring for them. Silly me, for some reason I thought when they grew past two or three years old, my duties wouldn't be so demanding or so daily. I quickly learned that while my arms may have been a bit more freed up, my time still wasn't.

It's not always easy to be a mom. Tucked not so neatly between the sweet cuddly moments of sheer awe are days and nights of frequent and inconvenient interruptions.

Whether you are queen of the scheduled life or you function better on the fly, your life as a mother is on high alert for incoming interruptions. It's just part of being a mom.

One mom recently said, "I never knew being a mom was the hardest job in the world! There are no breaks!"

Children cry in the middle of the night, sometimes for no apparent reason. They get sick, hurt and hungry. They have doctor's appointments, field trips, baseball practice and dance lessons. Moms learn to expect the unexpected, and love is sometimes demonstrated most when it is the least convenient.

In the real world, it's going to happen. Life often shows up at the most inconvenient times. The question is, how are you going to deal with it? How will love be your response when you're busy and burdened, frustrated and frazzled?

Like a boy scout who is always prepared, a momma with a good game plan is better equipped to deal with disruptions. Being equipped is like filling your toolbox with reactions to those little irritations and inconveniences you are sure to face each day.

The trick is remembering to pull your equipment out of your tool-box when it's time.

Recently, I watched what seemed to be a tale of two moms. Both had to deal with disruptions and interruptions, but each handled them very differently. One was prepared and one was not. The one who was prepared dealt with her circumstances better than the one who looked as if she was ready to blow a fuse.

Love isn't always convenient, but sometimes that's when it's demonstrated best. Ultimately, every time you choose to respond to your children's inconveniences in a loving way, you're laying your life down for theirs. You are laying your time and your plans down for theirs. You are laying your attitude down to develop their character. You are laying your anger down to instill patience and integrity in their hearts.

> By this we know love, that he laid down his life for us and we ought to lay down our lives for the brothers (1 John 3:16, *ESV*).

> Greater love has no one than this, that someone lay down his life for his friends (John 15:13, *ESV*).

When you lay your life down for those you claim to love, you ultimately demonstrate that you really do. Loving your children when it is inconvenient does not mean our world somehow revolves around theirs. It just means that when interruptions arise, we handle them in a way that displays our love for our children rather than our frustration at the situation.

In Real Life

As moms, we don't always do the right things. Sometimes our inconveniences can cause us to have a lapse in judgment. We've all heard of stories where a parent left his or her child in the car while running into the house to grab something or when stopping by a friend's house to pick something up or when dashing into a convenience store. It is only for a minute, but it's a minute that could change everything.

How often have we read headlines with very unhappy endings to lives that were devastated because someone chose the convenient over the crucial.

Recently I read an article about a precious mom whose life was forever changed because she chose the convenient over the crucial.

> Cassandra Alonzo was driving a 1995 Ford Explorer west-bound at 8 AM on Parkway Drive in the center lane next to the median. Her two daughters, Allessandra, 3, and Gabri-elle, 5, were riding in the back seat. . . . The SUV crossed the median onto eastbound traffic before it rolled. Allessandra was ejected from the vehicle and died at the scene. Both of the girls were not wearing seatbelts or in safety seats.[3]

Cassandra faces a lifetime of regret because she didn't take the time to buckle her children's seat belts. Perhaps a seatbelt would have saved her daughter's life. Perhaps it wouldn't have made any difference at all. Cassandra will never know if that one small in-convenient act might have possibly protected her precious child.

It's not always convenient to love our children. Mommas are constantly laying their lives down to do what is right—even when they are busy, burdened, frustrated or frazzled. Love is willing to forsake itself for the good of someone else. It's choosing to do what is best for others because we love them—even when it's inconvenient.

Loving in Their Language

De tal manera amó Dios al mundo, que ha dado a su Hijo unigénito, para que todo aquel que en él cree no se pierda, sino que tenga vida eterna.

Unless you speak Spanish, you have little or no idea what the above quote says. It is John 3:16—the greatest statement of love in the history of mankind; yet you don't understand what it says because it is not written in your language. Love is like that. Unless we show love to the ones we love in their love language, they don't really feel it, at least not to the extent we are trying to show it.

In 1997, Gary Chapman and Ross Campbell wrote a book that revolutionized the way we love our children. It's entitled *The Five Love Languages of Children* and it's definitely a must-read for every mother.

In the book, they list five ways a child gives and receives love. They are:

1. Physical Touch—A hug, a gentle touch, a pat on the back are all expressions of love to a child whose love language is physical touch.

2. Words of Affirmation—Expressing words of encouragement, praise, affection and acceptance all help validate your love for a child whose love language is words of affirmation.

3. Quality Time—Spending time with your child, hanging out together, watching TV together, intentionally being present when you are with them are all ways to say, "I love you," to the child whose love language is quality time.

4. Gifts—Giving that special gift, at just the right time, in just the right way, wrapped in just the right package are all ways to lavish your love on the one whose love language is gift giving. Big or small, it doesn't matter.

5. Acts of Service—Doing little things speaks volumes to the heart of a child whose love language is acts of service. Fixing a broken toy, making his favorite dessert, or sewing a button on her shirt are all ways to show your love.[4]

It's been said, "There ain't no love like a mother's love," but if Momma isn't loving her children in a way they understand, then they ain't feeling the love.

If your child's love language is acts of service and you shower them with gifts, your love is getting lost in translation. You can do your best to show them you love them, but they still may wonder why you don't. How sad to know that countless children feel unloved by mothers who love them immensely.

Here are a few tips to help you love each child well:

1. Notice how your children love. Pay attention to the ways they show affection to you, your family and their friends. Begin a chart that lists the five love languages and as you see your children loving others, write down the actions in the appropriate columns.

2. Take note of your children's likes and dislikes. If you give them a gift and they aren't impressed, then gift giving is not the way to show your love. If you sit at the table with them while they are doing their homework and they obviously enjoy your presence, then quality time speaks love to their little hearts.

3. Experiment with love. Consistently look for opportunities to love your children in every language. Take note of how they respond.

Your children have more than one love language. It's normal to have a primary and a secondary language. But finding out what is first and last on their list will completely revolutionize the way you love your child. I highly recommend *The Five Love Languages for Children* for every mother who is sincerely seeking to love her children well. You can also find several free resources online that will help you begin the journey at http://www.5lovelanguages.com/assessments/love/.

Love in Any Language

There may be five basic love languages but a simple smile, a lively laugh and positive words in a negative world are expressions of love in any language.

An accepting smile has a way of saying I love you without saying a word. A simple smile soothes hurting hearts and brings comfort, encouragement and acceptance to little hearts that are longing for your approval.

Laughing aloud brings people together. A good belly laugh is fun for the whole family! The Bible says that laughter is health to your bones. So help make your family a healthy one—laugh out loud—a lot!

Positive word choices shed positive light on negative circumstances. Children are bombarded with negative feedback from their parents and their peers. We will talk more about the power and effect of our words in chapter 6, but as mommas, let's allow love to flow through the words we choose.

Let no unwholesome word proceed from your mouth, but only such a word as is good for edification according to the need of the moment, so that it will give grace to those who hear (Eph. 4:29, *NASB*).

Loving your children is so much more than just feeling warm and fuzzy affection. It's intentionally loving them in a language they will understand, and when they understand you love them, it can make all the difference in the world.

Relentless Love

As the sun began to sneak a peek through the horizontal lines of my mini-blinds, I was reminded that another hectic day awaited me. It wasn't easy being an early bird and a night owl in the same skin, but as a single mom who was struggling to be all and do all, I didn't have many other options.

You're a momma, so you know all too well that each day holds its own basketful of burdens for a girl who wears too many hats. An overflowing to-do list is a constant in any mother's life. There is breakfast to cook, lunches to pack, daycare drop-offs and school bus pick-ups. There is dinner to prepare, a house to clean, laundry to wash and trips to the grocery store. There are doctor appointments, dentist appointments, field trips and open house. There are baseball practices, piano recitals, church plays and time to help with homework—not to mention a full-time job. With a list like that, a momma needs some rest—time to put her feet up and her head down—time to de-clutter her mind and de-stress her heart.

Did you know there is an annual holiday called "Lazy Mom's Day" held on September 3? It's a day of nothingness in honor of a year of everything-ness. A chill-fest of sorts. A day mommas can indulge in their quest for rest.

But we all know a mother's work is never done, so how do we love our little ones well when we're dead-dog tired and at the end of our proverbial rope? How can we prepare meals, make sure the kiddos are bathed, their teeth are brushed, their homework is done and we've tucked them in bed, when all we want to do is pull the covers over our heads?

Even discipline requires a relentless love. No means no—even when we're exhausted and we really want to say okay, but just this once. I'm not sure how, but children know that a tired mom almost equals a mushy mom.

Proverbs 24:30-31 provides an amazing parallel between what happens when a caretaker doesn't take care of his vineyard and what happens when mommas don't take care of their children:

> I walked by the field of a lazy person, the vineyard of one with no common sense. I saw that it was overgrown with nettles. It was covered with weeds, and its walls were broken down (*NLT*).

Your children are the vineyard of your life. The ones you are to nurture, feed, weed, prune and protect. But what happens when the vineyard's caretaker is no longer relentless?

Neglecting to Nurture—Gardens that are neglected become unkempt, uncontrollable and unpleasant. When a mom neglects to care for her children, they not only begin to feel abandoned, but they also behave much like that neglected garden. After all, if mom doesn't care, who does?

Failing to Feed—Last year, my husband and I planted some tomatoes. Unfortunately, my chaotic schedule consumed my time and I completely forgot to fertilize my precious backyard produce. Instead of a plethora of plump juicy tomatoes, my puny plants produced a stunted selection that fell off the vine before it was time.

When we are too tired to fertilize our children's hearts and minds with honesty, respect, righteousness, loyalty, consideration and compassion, we stunt their moral character and impede the growth of their integrity.

Too Weary to Weed—Children are like sponges. What they see they do. What they hear they say. You are their filter for right and wrong.

You weed through what they are exposed to and carefully choose what should take root and what should be eliminated.

Patience to Prune—When your day is done and so are you, there's always more. More meals to prepare, more dishes to wash, more clothes to clean and more homework to assist.

If you work outside the home, you know a 40-hour workweek has a way of zapping your energy as well as your resolve. Time with the kiddos must be intentional. When your children get too big for their britches (and they will), when you see them taking hold of ideas beyond their normal age limits, it's time to get the pruning shears out.

Pruning removes that which prevents the beautiful from emerging. Those distinctly inappropriate views and attitudes that seem to surface in a child's heart mean it's time for momma to start pruning.

Too Pooped to Protect—It's 6:30 PM and you just walked through the door with groceries in one hand and your child in the other. You still have a ton of work to do but you hear the bed calling your name and wish you could answer the call.

It's so easy to let television become your babysitter when your life is so busy. It's easy to become disengaged because your mind is on a thousand and one other things, but your little ones need you to protect their hearts and their minds.

It's not easy to always be on your game—to be diligent when you'd rather just crawl into bed, pull the covers over your head and call it a day. But love considers the needs of others more important than its own—even when it's tired, and so do moms who relentlessly seek to love their children well.

> Children are not casual guests in our home. They have been loaned to us temporarily for the purpose of loving them and instilling a foundation of values on which their future lives will be built.—James Dobson

A Lifestyle of Love

Somehow he always found my hiding place. No matter how hard I tried to hide the junk food, my youngest son made it his mission to discover where the goodies were stashed. I knew because the snacks would go missing and I would find empty crumpled-up packages between his mattress and in the bottom of his toy box.

My only option was to stop buying my own comfort food, but that would mean I would have to do without what I wanted and I wasn't really keen on giving up something I liked just because he had no self-control.

But isn't that what love is supposed to do? Sacrifice?

Healthy doesn't come easily in a world full of fast foods and prepackaged meals. Cars, couches and modern-day conveniences have made it much more difficult to stay active. We've become spectators instead of participants. Our lives are busy, our schedules are full and we are all running on empty.

Our children live in a generation that has never experienced daily trips to the playground or required physical education classes. Theirs has been a culture of computers, televisions and video games, with little or no exercise and lots of tasty, fat-filled snacks just a pantry door away.

No wonder childhood obesity has more than tripled in the past 30 years.[5] Over 13 percent of children are obese and that number is on the rise every year. Their health and emotional wellbeing are at risk. Children are now suffering from diabetes, high blood pressure, high cholesterol levels, sleep apnea and even heart problems, as well as low self-esteem, isolation and depression. They are the brunt of hurtful jokes and are frequently harassed by bullies. They are stared at, glared at and many times ignored.

Food becomes their friend when no one else will. It fills their time as well as their stomachs. Every bite amplifies their problem, yet it alleviates their hurting heart. They keep eating to mask the pain and fill a need that cannot be satisfied with food.

Teaching Self-control

I wish I could blame my mom's sweet tooth for my love of all things chocolate, but I was adopted. And while genetics can often be an indicator of future obesity, there is freedom in knowing that family habits have the power to redefine what was once thought to be inevitable.

Moms are in the control seat of a child's self-control. They have the opportunity to help their children establish healthy habits that will make their tomorrows much better than their family history would dictate. As moms, we get to instill healthy habits in their lives before they have a chance to develop bad ones on their own. Self-control is not only essential to healthy eating habits and physical activity, but it also strengthens our ability to exercise self-control in other areas.

If you are a Christian, Christ has made you more than a conqueror. You don't have to be held captive by anything or anyone. Romans 8:37 tells us that we are more than conquerors. In Titus 2:4-5, just on the heels of the call to teach women to love their husbands and children, mentors are given the daunting task of teaching women to exhibit self-control:

> Then they can urge the younger women to love their husbands and children, *to be self-controlled* and pure, to be busy at home, to be kind, and to be subject to their husbands, so that no one will malign the word of God (*NIV*, emphasis added).

We are human. Anger, impatience, intolerance, frustration, word choices, attitudes, as well as eating right and exercising regularly are issues with which we all have struggled. Self-control is something we all need. It's one of the fruits of the Spirit listed in Galatians 5:22-23:

> But the Holy Spirit produces this kind of fruit in our lives: love, joy, peace, patience, kindness, goodness, faithfulness, gentleness, and *self-control*. There is no law against these things! (*NLT*, emphasis added).

Self-controlled mommas can teach their children to have self-control, not just by what they say but also by how they live!

None of us can be Supermom. When our children come into the world, we aren't given a golden lasso along with their birth certificates. But we are given relatives, friends, books and mentors to help us in our journey.

This book is meant to be a tool to help you in your journey, but it's important to remember that there are no cookie-cutter families. What works in one family may not work in another. But when it's all said and done, you can't go wrong when you truly love your children well.

Summing It Up

As much as I've wanted to, I haven't always loved my children well. No mother has. You can know all the right answers and make your "How to Be a Loving Mom" list all you want, but when your child dives to the floor in the middle of the store and begins kicking and screaming, your patience can become as elusive as your "Loving Mom" list.

This chapter on love is not meant to overwhelm you with a multitude of mandates, but hopefully it will help you be a proactive rather than a reactive parent—one who loves her children well.

A Prayer for Mom

Oh wow, Lord! Love is so much more than a four-letter word with a two-word definition and I'm desperate for You to help me love my children well. How beautifully You define love in 1 Corinthians 13. Please help my love for my children look like that in real life. Help me to love them when it's inconvenient, to love them in a language they will understand, to love them by being firm when I need to be firm and by being gentle and loving at all times, and by loving them enough to not only take care of them but also to take care of myself.

More for Mom

Love Is . . .

1. How did your definition of love change after you completed this "How Do I Love Thee?" chapter?
2. Do you have anything in your background that might cause you to struggle with understanding, giving or accepting love?

3. Have you seen a mother's love demonstrated well by other moms, and if so, what did that look like?
4. How can 1 Corinthians 13:4-8 become a way to test your actions as a mom?

An Inconvenient Love
5. Tragedies often happen when children are neglected. What are some decisions you can make to prevent a tragedy happening with your own children?
6. Why is it so important to love your children, even when it's inconvenient?

Loving in Their Language
7. What is your personal love language?
8. How would you explain the importance of learning your child's love language?
9. If you don't know your child's love language, what are some things you can do to discover his or her love language and then begin to demonstrate love to them in a language they'll understand?

Relentless Love
10. Do you struggle with giving up or giving in when it comes to your children?
11. How does the illustration of caring for a vineyard relate to parenting your child?

A Lifestyle of Love
12. Many people struggle with self-control in a variety of ways. What are some areas where you struggle with self-control?
13. Some people don't really know how to prepare healthy meals or start an exercise program. If this is something you struggle with, what are some ways you can discover healthy recipes so that your children can develop healthy eating habits? How can you implement a daily dose of exercise (or play) in your children's day as well as in your own?

Summing It Up

14. How has this chapter changed or challenged your thoughts about how a mother loves her children?
15. What are some ways you can begin loving your kids well today?

Notes

1. *Holman Illustrated Bible Dictionary*, 2003 Holman Bible Publishers.
2. Ibid.
3. Gabrielle Monte, "Unrestrained Child Dies in Morning Car Accident," *Lubbock Avalanche-Journal*, July 14, 2006. http://lubbockonline.com/stories/071406/loc_071406056.shtml (accessed January 2014).
4. Gary Chapman, Ph.D., and Ross Campbell, M.D., *The Five Love Languages of Children* (Chicago: Northfield, 1997).
5. "Childhood Obesity Facts," Centers for Disease Control and Prevention, July 10, 2013. http://www.cdc.gov/HealthyYouth/obesity/ (accessed January 2014).

5

MAY I HAVE YOUR ATTENTION?

Direct your children onto the right path,
and when they are older, they will not leave it.
PROVERBS 22:6, *NLT*

How can moms create a healthy balance between too much and not enough attention when real life can be so messy? How can she know if she's giving her kids too much or not enough attention? "May I Have Your Attention?" helps mothers find the balance between giving their children the attention they need to develop a proper view of themselves while avoiding the dilemma of creating self-centered children and child-centered homes.

The Mom with the Kids

I had seen her before at events gone by. She was always fun to be around and conversation with her was easy. But when her children were with her, it was a different story. Oh, she was still fun and conversation was still easy, but her kids were a handful and hanging out with her when her kids were around was like getting in a bouncy house with a dozen cats. They were loud, out of control and nerve-wracking.

Every plate of food that had been carefully and creatively positioned on display for the evening event would soon be pillaged by her kids as they poked their slobber-laden fingertips into each one. The punch bowl was transformed into a spittoon as her oldest son would dunk his cup deep into the bowl, take a taste, spit it back into the cup and then pour it back into the punch bowl. The beautiful decorations became toys in her children's hands, and the noise level peaked at penetrating proportions with shrieks from her playful kiddos.

Their momma was a precious woman who was loved by all, but she was often distracted and disengaged from her children—those with whom she was entrusted and called to raise. Tuning out those tiny tots had become the norm for her. She no longer only filtered out their petty chatter, but she also became absent, even when she was present. Most mommas have an innate ability to tune out the trivial. They can tell whether a child's cry is solely for attention because he's tired or hungry or because there is a legitimate need. It's really just a mom thing. But when a mother gets into the habit of turning a deaf ear and a blind eye to her children, she can become dangerously disengaged from the ones who need her most. You see, sweet mom, we can be present and yet be very absent. Proverbs 29:15 warns us that a child left to himself will cause a mother shame.

Whether a mother works a full-time job or is a stay-at-home mom, the propensity is there to become preoccupied with everything but her children. Bill Cosby once said, "Raising a teenager is like nailing Jell-O to the wall." Giving our kids the right amount of attention is just as hard and often just as messy. It's tough being a mom, and with so many things vying for our attention, it's becoming increasingly difficult for moms to focus on their kids. Today's moms are busier and, unfortunately, more distracted than ever.

The pressure to be Pinterest-perfect moms is relentless. Moms who show up at *every* play day, *every* practice, *every* game, and *every* birthday party with their children in perfectly matched clothes and just the right gifts can be daunting.

The mom life is hard and moms are crazy busy. With overflowing to-do lists, crayon-colored walls, dishes that just won't go away, a laundry pile on steroids, kids tugging at them for their time, and for many the demands of a part-time or full-time job, moms are finding it hard just to catch their breath. It's tough to juggle life with so many balls in the air at one time.

Some moms are so sidetracked by life that they find it hard to focus on their kids. Other moms struggle with being disconnected from their kids when others are around. Some mothers find that time with their friends is more fun and less taxing. Others are just tired of the relentless responsibilities parenting requires. It's easier to disengage than to deal with the overwhelming demands of motherhood. Some moms have found that the virtual world at their fingertips is much more pleasurable than the real world being lived out right under their noses.

Recently, I was in a doctor's office waiting room where I observed a common modern-day phenomenon. It was a mom frantically fidgeting with her cell phone—constantly checking for the last email, latest text and newest Facebook post from her friends.

Her chatty children were the last thing on her mind and they seemed to be frustrated, let down and left out. Mom was far too busy with her virtual world to be fully present in her real world. She was a dangerously distracted and disengaged mom. It's not just teens who have a tendency to become addicted to all things tech. It's not only teenagers whom we worry about because they text while driving, are consistently oblivious to the conversation others are having with them, and are completely unaware of the real life that is taking place right before their eyes. Mommas have joined the ranks of the virtual world on the World Wide Web and are just as captivated by the cyber life as their kids.

In a world where, through technology, we are more connected than ever before, we are also less connected than we have ever been. Navigating the tech trap and the social media mania that have captivated the hearts of this generation is seemingly just as difficult for moms as it is for the children they are raising.

Social media and technology are amazing. We are able to meet people we would never meet otherwise. There is more information at our fingertips now than when I was a child and a family's idea of the information highway was a complete set of the *Encyclopedia Britannica* and a *Webster's Dictionary*.

But technology seems to have complicated things. What was meant to make life easier has captivated the hearts and minds of mommas who already have a ton of things to do. It is a dangerous thing when moms are more connected to their friends on Facebook than they are with their kids. And when children aren't able to garner their momma's attention, there is a world out there that will pay attention to them.

Now, more than ever, moms have to be much more intentional about being present when they are present. If they don't, they will neglect giving their children the attention they so desperately need. However, giving a child too much attention can have the opposite effect. Many moms struggle with allowing their world to revolve around their child's every whim, creating a self-centered child and a child-centered home.

Jacob and Esau

In Genesis 25:21-34 we find a tale of two brothers: Jacob and Esau. They were twins whose battle for attention began in the womb. When it was time to be born, there was a battle for who would be firstborn. Esau managed to secure a place at the front of the line as Jacob grabbed Esau's heal in a last failed effort to steal his spot.

The Bible goes on to say, "So the boys grew. And Esau was a skillful hunter, a man of the field; but Jacob was a mild man, dwelling in tents. And Isaac loved Esau because he ate of his game, but Rebekah loved Jacob" (Gen. 25:27-28). Embedded in verse 28 is the painful and destructive dynamic of what happens when one child is preferred above another. It's sibling rivalry at its worst and it happens in the best of homes.

The twins lived in the same home and experienced equal, yet reverse realities. Esau received too much attention from his daddy, Isaac, and not enough from his momma, Rebekah. Jacob was the apple of his momma's eye, but he was desperate for his daddy's attention. The boys were pitted against each other and frustrated by favoritism. Theirs was a child-centered home where both children longed for attention from a parent who only had eyes for the other child. When parents play favorites, nobody wins.

Having the attention and affection of only one parent leaves a child longing for the same from the other parent. It's like a cup that is half full. That same cup is just as much half empty—and so is a child who is the center of one parent's universe and barely exists in the other parent's world.

That was Jacob and Esau's reality, and the result was a show-down for first place—a battle to become the heir not only to their daddy's estate but to his blessings as well. What started in the womb ended with a savory bite of lentil stew. Esau, hungry for food; Jacob, starving for the rights of the firstborn. They made an exchange they thought would satisfy them both, but it only proved to leave each empty.

The battle may have been over, but the war was just beginning. After the family picked up their tent and moved to Gerar, Esau's disregard for his family became obvious. At 40 years of age, he decided to do his own thing, and contrary to everything his parents had taught him, he married Hittite wives.

> When Esau was forty years old, he took Judith the daughter of Beeri the Hittite to be his wife, and Basemath the daughter of Elon the Hittite, and they made life bitter for Isaac and Rebekah (Gen. 26:34, *ESV*).

It's one of the consequences of a child-centered home. You give those little bundles of joy their way all the time and they grow up thinking they can do whatever they want. To them, rules are made to be broken. Boundaries are for everyone else. They become their own idol because their parents have made them theirs. As daddy's little favorite, that's exactly what Esau did. And he brought grief to his parents.

Then there was Jacob. Momma's boy. The one who in the womb jockeyed for the position of firstborn and later won it with a bowl of soup wasn't alone in his fight for first place. His doting mother added her own dose of deception to the plot in order to shore up Jacob's lead.

Daddy Isaac was growing old and knew it was time to pass down the blessing of the firstborn. So he sent his favorite son, Esau, to hunt a bite for him to eat. He did not realize his eavesdropping wife was concocting a cunning plan:

> She said to her son Jacob, "Listen. I overheard your father say to Esau, 'Bring me some wild game and prepare me a delicious meal. Then I will bless you in the Lord's presence

before I die.' Now, my son, listen to me. Do exactly as I tell you. Go out to the flocks, and bring me two fine young goats. I'll use them to prepare your father's favorite dish. Then take the food to your father so he can eat it and bless you before he dies." "But look," Jacob replied to Rebekah, "my brother, Esau, is a hairy man, and my skin is smooth. What if my father touches me? He'll see that I'm trying to trick him, and then he'll curse me instead of blessing me." But his mother replied, "Then let the curse fall on me, my son! Just do what I tell you. Go out and get the goats for me!" (Gen. 27:6-13, *NLT*).

Rebekah got much more than she bargained for when her ploy for her favorite son produced a lot more problems than she had planned. Oh, he did as she said and received the blessing of the first-born, but her words became her curse and after she and Isaac sent her precious Jacob running for his life, she would never see him again.

The one who had become the center of her world was now just a memory and all that was left were the pieces of her broken heart and their broken home.

Rebekah—the same barren woman who was given a child when Isaac prayed for her—was now dealing with barrenness of another kind. With Jacob gone forever, her heart was as empty as her arms.

A wise woman builds her home, but a foolish woman tears it down with her own hands (Prov. 14:1, *NLT*).

Because she favored one son over another, Rebekah tore her own home down with her hands. Eventually, Jacob and Esau made amends, but what they had lost could never be regained. Their broken family defined "dysfunctional." Sweet memories of playful days and BBQ dinners in the backyard would never be again. Holiday dinners and the laughter of children and grandchildren echoing through the air would never exist. It had all been lost somewhere between the pride of two brothers and their parents' preferences.

That story happened over 4,000 years ago but it still happens today in homes around the world. Children with mounting insecurities strive for attention and feel invisible in their own homes. Other children think the world begins and ends with them. One is an attention-starved child. The other is a child who rules the roost in a child-centered home. Some, like Jacob and Esau, experience both.

Unfortunately, it is all too common to bond with one child more than with another. Somewhere in the messiness of motherhood, we try our best to divvy out our love and attention in equal proportions, but it's not easy. Personalities have a way of drawing us closer to one child or making us feel detached and distant from another.

I wish there was some kind of simple solution to solve the problem of too much or not enough attention. But there's not. Each child is unique. Each one responds to life, love and all things in between very differently. What works for one will not work for the other. Their personalities, passions and purposes are different. One will wear you out, one will wear you down and another will make parenting seem like a day at the park.

My boys have always been very different. My oldest was drawn to anything sports and didn't require an overwhelming amount of attention. He was happy with a basketball in one hand and a football in the other. But because he didn't seem to need much attention, I had to be careful not to neglect giving him the little attention he did need.

It's easy to become accustomed to the fact that your child doesn't demand your attention and to start taking his easy-going personality for granted. The need for little attention does not equal the need for *no* attention.

Paying Attention to the Attention Needs of Your Children

I remember one year when both my boys played ball. Karl, who was 13, had a game at one park, and DJ, who was 7, had to be at practice at another park. My hubby was working, so I had to get both to games.

I dropped Karl off at his game and took DJ to practice where I waited until practice was over. Then I rushed back to Karl's game, but when I arrived I noticed my little man sitting on the bench, fighting back tears that were puddling in his eyes.

At first, I thought he had been hurt. But as I ran to the dugout, and in true mommy form, yelled, "What's wrong? Are you okay?" He quietly gazed at the ground and whispered, "I hit a triple, Mom . . . and you missed it."

My brave little man, who never seemed to need anything from his momma, was broken-hearted that I wasn't there to see him score a big hit for the team. My heart sank as I stood there with nothing to say but "I'm *so* sorry!"

Because Karl didn't need a lot of attention, it was sometimes easy to forget that he still needed some attention—especially when it came to things that were important to him. My little guy was left to wonder why his momma had forgotten to give him the attention he needed.

If I could turn back the hands of time, I would have been at that game. It meant a lot to him and DJ could have cared less about being at practice. I think he ran the bases backward anyway.

I learned a lot that day as my fingers gripped the chain link fence and my heart melted in my chest. I learned that a bad day didn't make me a bad mom. I also learned that being intentional with my attention was a necessary part of loving my kids well.

DJ was another story. He thrived on lots of attention. He longed for me to notice just about everything he did, and when I didn't, he made sure I knew about it. It was definitely a delicate balance to give him the attention he needed without making him think our world revolved around him. At times, we ended up leaning too far to one side or the other, and it was a constant challenge to find a healthy attention-zone, somewhere between too much and not enough.

We didn't always get it right. No parent does. We weren't always sure of the right thing to do. No parent is. But a momma has to pay attention to the attention needs of her children as well as guard her heart against favoring one child over another. If not, she will discover that she has created an attention-starved child or a child-centered home.

Tara's Story

For Tara, divvying up the attention on any given day isn't easy. Tara is a mother of five kids. One is an adopted child with special needs from a brain injury due to the fact that his birth mom did drugs; another child has juvenile diabetes; and three boys—one of whom is already with the Lord from Trisomy 18. For Tara and the multitude of moms who have special needs kids, it's even more difficult to find a good balance on the attention scale.

When her daughter Lynnie's eyes rolled back in her head and her face morphed into a pale blue-grey, Tara knew her blood sugar was dangerously low. While desperately digging through the drawer to find the emergency glucose kit, Tara heard a familiar scream from the next room. It was her eight-year-old, developmentally disabled daughter throwing her five o'clock fit because of an irrational phobia she had of bathrooms.

Somewhere between the record-breaking shrills coming from the other room and her frantic attempts to find the glucose kit, Tara's other two boys darted through the kitchen and blurted out, "Hey, Mom! What's for dinner?" They were completely unaware of the chaos going on around them, or maybe just so used to it that they didn't care. Boys with hungry bellies have a tendency to miss the obvious anyway.

How can Tara meet every child's needs when they are all calling for her at the same time? How can she measure out attention when the urgent takes precedence over the important? How can you—and I—create a healthy balance between too much and not enough attention when real life can be so messy?

There is no answer that fits every home, every situation, every family or every child. One size doesn't fit all. That's true in life. That's true in each family. And while it's important to remember that children may be as different as a box of chocolates, it's also important to note that there are certain threads that run through the fabric of every home with an attention-starved child as well as every child-centered home.

It's true that kids need attention—lots of it. They are growing up and developing into the people God created them to be. They need to be nurtured along the way. They need direction, correction, protection and interaction. I struggled to find the fine line between the two. At times, I was on target. Other times, I completely missed the mark.

We all want to be good moms, but finding the elusive balance we so desperately need to be the best moms we can is not only challenging but also sometimes scary. Too much attention is just as bad as too little.

There Is Hope

So, how does a mom know whether she has an attention-starved child or a child-centered home?

Let's begin by looking at some distinguishing characteristics of an attention-starved child. Your little one might be desperate for your attention if:

- He creates a disturbance to get your attention.
- He's noticeably loud and even obnoxious.
- He cries, pouts or whines a lot.
- He withdraws from others.
- He shows signs of depression.
- He exhibits unreasonable, unexplainable and/or uncontrollable anger.
- He becomes rebellious.
- He tells you he feels that you are neglecting him.

You may be thinking, *I see all of the above and more in my child!* But seeing it occasionally isn't the same as it becoming a pattern in your child's behavior. You're looking for patterns, not periodic outbursts or random bouts with attitudes.

If you begin to see your child exhibiting some of these behaviors, there are some things you can do to put the brakes on the attention deficit your child is experiencing:

1. Start with yourself. Consider what has been captivating your attention and begin making some adjustments to free up your time and attention.
2. If you have more than one child, use bedtime as a bonding time. Try to stagger your children's bedtimes with the youngest being first, and so on. That will enable you to spend a few valuable minutes one on one with each child.
3. Love languages matter. When you want to reinforce how much you love them, don't let your efforts get lost in translation. Love them in a way they will receive it best.

4. Be creative. Go to a park, play outside, have a play date with the kiddos, play a board game together, take your child out for ice cream, go to the library together, bake a cake for the family or cupcakes for school or for Sunday school class together, go to the beach or hiking together. Do something. Do anything. But just spend some individual time with your child. You'll be surprised what a difference it will make.

There are a ton of ways to show your children how important they are to you, but with life tugging hard at your time and the needs of your kids tugging hard on your heart, something's got to give and it can't be your children. The attention you give your kids is an investment in their character, self-esteem and future. A momma has to be intentional about attention. But a child who has had too much attention is a disaster waiting to happen.

So, how do you know if your child is just behaving badly or if you have a child-centered home on your hands?

You might have a child-centered home if:

- Your child throws temper tantrums to get his/her way.
- Your child yells at you, screams when you tell him/her no or tells you he/she hates you.
- Your child tells you no consistently and demonstrates disrespect to you and other adults.
- Your child tries to tell you what to do.
- Your child expects to get his/her way.
- Your child doesn't follow or respect rules.
- Your child is selfish, rude and argumentative.
- You cower to your child's demands.
- You are afraid of upsetting your child when you tell him/her no.
- Your schedule revolves around your child's whims.
- You jump when your child tells you he/she wants something.

Children who dominate a home wreak havoc on relationships with family and friends. It's an uncomfortable and unnatural role reversal that is humiliating and debilitating for the parents. Just remember, you're the momma, so *be* the momma! You don't have to be controlled by a 4-year-old or a 14-year-old. You have the authority to be in authority and your kids will be much better off when you take the lead.

Sweet momma, if you have somehow allowed your attention-demanding little one to rule the roost, you know the strain it's causing your family. You don't have to be held captive to their demands or attitudes any longer.

Here are a few things you can do to regain control:

- Set rational boundaries and stick to your stuff. Don't allow your child to manipulate you through an extreme pouting fest or a temper tantrum gone wild. You're the mom, so you can remain calm and in control even if your child doesn't.
- Don't lose it. You are setting an example every time you act and react to your child's misbehavior. If you want them to control themselves, you control yourself.
- Look for opportunities to teach them patience, kindness and self-control. Sometimes these words don't mean much to children, so give them examples of what each looks like when lived out in real life by pointing out these character traits when you see them demonstrated by others. Don't forget to make sure they see what the opposite behaviors in others look like as well.
- Let your child fail. Children need to learn about consequences, struggles and how to deal with adversity. You may need to help them through it, but don't help them out of it.
- Don't go overboard. You may have a tendency to place too many rules and restrictions on your child because you want to teach him/her who's boss. Make reasonable rules and be consistent with the ones you make. Consistency is really the key.

A Prayer for Mom

Father, I confess there is a very fine line between giving my children too much attention and not giving them enough. It's not always easy to know the right thing to do and it's definitely not easy to always do what I know is right. Precious Father, please give me the wisdom to discern the level of attention my children need to thrive without going

*overboard and making them the center of my world. Help me be
intentional with the attention I give them and enable me to create
an environment in my home where we never play favorites and
where all my children feel equally loved and significant.*

❋ More for Mom

The Mom with the Kids
1. Have you known a precious mom who was distracted and disengaged from her kids?
2. How do you think that made her children feel?
3. What are some areas where you need to be careful so that you don't become a distracted and disengaged momma?

Jacob and Esau
4. Why do you think it is easy for parents to gravitate to one child or the other?
5. What lessons can you learn from Jacob and Esau that will help you become a better mom?
6. Do any of your children feel that you favor one child over another?

Paying Attention to the Attention Needs of Your Children
7. Does one of your children seem to require more attention than the other?
8. How can you deal with each child's attention needs in a healthy way?

Tara's Story
9. Why is it more difficult to balance the attention in a home with special needs kids?
10. What are some ways a mom who has special needs kids can assure her other kids that they are equally important and equally loved?
11. What are some ways others you know can help families where there are special needs kids so that the parents can spend some quality time with their other kids?

There Is Hope

12. Does your child exhibit behavior that is typical of an attention-starved child or a child-centered home?
13. Were any of the tips helpful, and if so, which ones do you need to implement to help find a balance of attention in your home?

> Fathers, do not exasperate your children; instead, bring them up in the training and instruction of the Lord (Eph. 6:4, *NIV*).

6

SPEAKING WORDS OF WISDOM

A word fitly spoken is like apples of gold in a setting of silver.
PROVERBS 25:11, *ESV*

"Cindy! Why don't you ever do what you're told?" Children are exposed to all sorts of words and comments. Words that wound. Comments that cut. Yet, no words have more impact than those of a mother. Unfortunately, moms don't always say the right things. Hormones rage, tempers flare and words don't always come out right. "Speaking Words of Wisdom" will help mothers gain the proper perspective of the power of their words while challenging them to think before they speak. This chapter is chock-full of practical word choices that will speak life rather than death into a child's life.

Wielding Your Words Well

I noticed her at the corner table in the restaurant with a cell phone to her ear and completely unaware of anything going on around her. Beside her was a little boy who looked to be about three or four years old. He kept tugging at the blouse of his very distracted mommy, but she acted as if he wasn't even there.

He started calling her name, but she just kept talking on the phone. After about the fifteenth time that precious little boy called out to his mommy, she whipped her head around and gave him one of the angriest faces I have ever seen. And without even thinking about where she was, she began yelling at her little guy, cussing at him and calling him terrible names. "Are you so #@# stupid that you can't see I'm talking? What in the #@# is wrong with you? Shut the #@# up! I've got an important phone call and I don't have time for you to interrupt me!"

I sat there, glaring at her with my mouth wide open, wanting to say something but not knowing what to say. And then I saw that sweet baby boy peering down and tears dropping off his little chubby cheeks. I couldn't believe what I was seeing, but in that single incident that momma managed to wound her son's heart with her words in a way that would most likely last a lifetime. And all he wanted to do was tell her he needed to go potty. Every time that momma chided her child, you could almost see his heart shriveling up. That day in the restaurant, that momma left scars on his heart that a Band-Aid could never cover up.

The scary thing about it is that if she would do that in public, what would she do in private? I'm sure that little fella had battle scars on his heart from a multitude of times that momma has wounded him with her words.

Being a momma is hard and we don't always say and do the right thing, but our words carry a lot of weight, so we must choose to use them wisely. The words we use can become weapons, and our tongues can be like swords—slicing and dicing to the very core of the human soul and leaving the recipient of our not-so-cleverly-crafted words wounded for life.

The good news is that our words can also be like an instrument playing the most beautiful sound in the world and echoing for a lifetime in the heart of the one to whom we are speaking. The words we choose have the power to speak life, to give courage, confidence and peace. What we say can speak hope and healing into a hurting heart. Our words can be balm on a broken heart, or a cool, soft breeze for a weary soul. The words that flow from a momma's lips are probably the most powerful of all, and learning to wield our words well is not for the faint of heart.

Lori's Story

When Lori's daughter was about a year old, Lori was concerned about her daughter's language development. The language clinician didn't seem to think anything was wrong, but as a first-time momma, Lori was worried that something wasn't right.

Lori and her husband continued seeking help for about a year and as it turned out, there really was an issue. When her daughter was two, she underwent a battery of tests and the results concluded that their precious baby girl was aphasic.

The language clinician sat Lori and her hubby down and began to explain that when someone is aphasic it means they are incapable of understanding language or forming words. It is most often associated with some sort of brain damage.

As they sat there trying to process the diagnosis and her prognosis, their hearts couldn't believe their ears. "Mr. and Mrs. Wildenberg, your daughter is aphasic and you need to prepare yourselves. Your daughter will never be able to go to regular school, do math, graduate from high school, or hold a job."

Their first response was, "*Nope*. Not our kid!" and they left determined that their diagnosis would not become their daughter's destiny. They knew God was *way* bigger than what the language clinician was telling them, and with His help, they were determined to win the war that seemed to be waged against their daughter's future.

They all worked very hard to help their little girl find her voice. They spoke life into her heart and when the battle seemed to be the most difficult, they continued to relentlessly walk by faith.

They said things like, "Mommy and Daddy are confident you can do this!" "You are strong and you can conquer this!" "You can do all things through Christ who gives you strength!"

They never allowed her to use her challenges as an excuse. They didn't focus on what she couldn't do, but they focused on how the Lord could help her overcome this challenge. They helped her understand that what she was going through would make her stronger and would only serve to solidify her spirit of tenacity.

Contrary to the language clinician's diagnosis, their precious little girl's language was delayed, but she was able to talk. By the time she was in kindergarten, she was able to begin her new journey in school as one of the better readers. In high school, she not only was able to read music and play various instruments, but she was also in the marching band.

Academics didn't come easily. It was a struggle for them all. But with a lot of leading from the Lord, a lot of hard work and perseverance and a relentless pursuit to pour words of encouragement into their little girl's life, their daughter graduated high school and is a bright and talented young lady.

Lori and her hubby wielded their words wisely. They gave their daughter the confidence she needed and the faith to believe her life could be so much more than a language clinician's diagnosis.

Parents have the power of speaking life into their children's lives to help them live beyond anyone else's critical comments or limiting concepts.

Kind words are like honey—sweet to the soul and healthy for the body (Prov. 16:24, *NLT*).

Lori and her hubby brought health to their little girl's heart and body by choosing their words wisely. And you and I can too.

Genny's Story

After working out at the gym one day, Genny got a powerful reminder of how potent her words could be. She made her way to the play area were her little ones were playing with the toys. When she passed by the window to the room where they were, her daughter, Katie, spotted her through the glass.

With her arms waving in the air, Katie began jumping up and down. Genny opened the door, looked into the room and there her precious girl was with a smile that looked like sunshine on her face. She ran to Genny with her arms open wide, grabbed her legs and shrilled, "*Mommy!*"

Genny had only been working out for about an hour, but her little girl was acting like she hadn't seen her momma in a week. What a way to melt a momma's heart! It made Genny think about how she greeted her little girl.

Genny pushed the rewind button of her mind and started reflecting on the morning before when she woke her daughter up with a quick kiss on the forehead and then shifted into fifth gear. "Hurry now! Don't take too long getting ready because it's our day to carpool. And you need to clean your room before we leave. It looks like a tornado came through here."

She remembered that when she had picked up her children from school, she rushed them along toward home right past the swings and a group of kids buying ice cream from the ice-cream truck. Basketball practice was the pressing priority on Genny's mind and she was so focused on getting there on time that she barely noticed how disappointed they were.

For Genny, each memory was a powerful reminder of how important her words are. Even how she says hi to her kids and the tone she uses when she speaks to them are ways that she conveys that she is focused on them instead of her to-do list.

When I was younger, my mom always said, "It's not always what you say, it's how you say it." That day after a good workout, a cherished hug from her happy little girl and a short walk down memory lane, Genny discovered that it's not only what you say but also how you say it that matters most to little hearts who hang on every word their momma says.

Proverbs 15:4 (*NLT*) tells us, "Gentle words are a tree of life." I can't help but wonder how many times I stunted my kids' emotional and spiritual growth by the things I said and the way I said them. Genny took stock of her words while her kids were young and worked hard at being intentional with what she said and how she said it.

What a wise momma!

The Power of Our Words

Recently, I asked some friends what was the worst thing anyone had ever said to them and why. I was flooded with heartbreaking stories of lives that had been wounded by words from days gone by; cutting comments that left scars on the hearts of precious people who still struggle to believe they are more than what someone said about them.

One sweet mom told me the most painful thing anyone ever said to her was that God should have given her kids a different mom. Another woman was told she would never be any good. From many, the cruel comments came from their parents. Comments like, "You were a mistake!" "You need to know that your brother is my favorite and always will be!" "I don't care that you made all *A*s; you should have made *A*-pluses!" "I wish you were never born!" "I should have aborted you!" "You're not very smart, are you?" "You will never be worth anything!" "I hate you!" "Get out! I never want to see you again!" "You are not my child anymore!" "You're too fat and no one is going to love you!"

Words can hurt. In fact, they can kill. Proverbs 18:21 (*KJV*) says, "Death and life are in the power of the tongue."

Perhaps like me and some of my precious friends who shared the painful words of their past, you have been the recipient of death words and you know how they can crush your spirit, derail your dreams, skew your self-image and hurt your heart.

Maybe you don't see yourself as you really are because you believed what someone told you, saying you were someone or something you really aren't. Oh, sweet friends, I wish I could hug every one of you reading this right now, because I know what it's like to find yourself somewhere in the middle of believing you are who and what others have said about you rather than trusting you are exactly who Christ has created you to be. The place where you try with your heart to believe with your head what you know to be true because Jesus said it was true, but you can't get past the painful impression embedded in your heart that makes you feel invisible, inadequate, incapable and inferior.

In life, our words count. As a mom, you have the power to speak life into the little life God has given you, but perhaps you need to find some healing for your own heart first. If you have been hurt by a callous, critical and cruel person, take some time and immerse yourself in the Word of the Living God. It is there as you allow Scripture to speak life into your life that you will find the truth about who you are. It's time to let God's Word be louder than anyone else's. It is *Jehovah-Rapha*, the Lord who heals, who tells us we were created in His image—fearfully and wonderfully made—that we are perfect in His sight—complete in Him. We are the objects of His affection, the apple of His eye and inscribed upon the palms of His hands. Sweet momma, it doesn't get any better than that! So, please don't you dare believe you are anything less than what our Savior died to make you!

We know the pain words can cause. We've all been the recipient of far too many callous comments. I know that pretty much every mom on the planet has said something to her kids that she shouldn't. Whether out of anger, arrogance or ignorance, we've all cut our kids with our sharp tongues. But we don't have to be the ones who hurt the hearts of our kids.

Words are kind of like food. What we take in can be sweet and nourishing or it can be bitter and make us sick. We choose what we eat, but whatever goes in must come out. So, to help us in our choice of words that will speak life into our kids and into the lives of those we come in contact with, let's evaluate a few Scriptures and see what the Word says about our words. Let's wage war on our loose lips and defeat the need to say more than we should. Let's do a little Q & A and learn some tips that can help us think before we speak.

In Luke 12:3 (*ESV*), the Bible says, "Therefore whatever you have spoken in the dark will be heard in the light, and what you have spoken in the ear in inner rooms will be proclaimed on the housetops."

What will be proclaimed on the housetops? Everything that is said where you think no one else will hear it. So, if what you are getting ready to say isn't something you would want shouted from a housetop, then it's best not to say it.

Ephesians 4:29 tells us, "Let no corrupt word proceed out of your mouth, but what is good for necessary edification, that it may impart grace to the hearers."

What kinds of words should be coming out of our mouths?

If you use Ephesians 4:29 as a filter for your words, you will be much less likely to wound your children's hearts with your words, and much more likely to choose words that will build them up.

Ephesians 5:4 in the *Amplified Bible* says, "Let there be no filthiness (obscenity, indecency) nor foolish *and* sinful (silly and corrupt) talk, nor coarse jesting, which are not fitting or becoming; but instead voice your thankfulness [to God]."

If your words could be described as obscene, indecent, foolish or corrupt, that's a strong indicator you need to change your word choices. Start using your voice to demonstrate a heart of thankfulness and you will begin to speak a whole new language.

There are a host of other verses that deal with the issue of our words. The words we speak are powerful. They have the ability to speak life or death into another person's life, especially our kids. If you've ever been hurt by hurtful words, you know how it feels. You may not be able to control what others say, but you have the power, through the Spirit of the Living God, to overcome an unbridled tongue.

Today, I pray you will evaluate your word choices to your husband, your children, your family members, your friends and your co-workers. Are you speaking life into theirs or are you wounding them with your words? Are you stirring the pot and causing division or are you speaking peaceful words of encouragement and forgiveness?

Practically Speaking

Jacqueline Kennedy Onassis is quoted to have said, "If you bungle raising your children, I don't think whatever else you do well matters very much."

A momma's words can lift a child beyond his or her wildest imagination or they can bring a child down into a pit so deep that he or she can't seem to climb out. Every word we speak and every action we take make all the difference in the world to a child who was born longing to sense a momma's love.

It has been said that for every one thing someone says that breaks a child's heart, that child needs to hear at least five positive things to counter that one negative comment. So, as a way to help us all choose words that speak healing to our children, here are some words we should and should not say:

Words that Speak Life	Words that Speak Death
You can do it!	You'll never be able to do it!
I'm sorry!	It was your fault I acted like that!
You're such a gift!	I wish you were never born!
I'm so thankful for you!	Would you just leave me alone!
It's okay! I've made mistakes too!	Why can't you do anything right?
You aren't the sum of your failures!	You're such a failure!

Words that Speak Life	Words that Speak Death
You can be anything you want!	You'll never be anything!
You aren't what others say about you! God defines you!	You're such a pain!
I believe in you!	You can't do that!
This will help you be stronger!	You deserve to go through it!
Who you are is what gives you value!	You never will be enough!
I don't know, but let's find out together!	Just don't worry about it!
Nothing could ever make me love you less!	I can't stand you!
You're so smart!	You're so stupid!
We can do this together!	I don't have time for you!
How can I help you with that?	That's a ridiculous hobby!
You are a priceless creation of God!	You are always in my way!

It's not always easy to say the right thing. We've all had hormonal meltdowns and mommy mess-ups. We've all said things we wish would have never come out of our mouths. We've said things to our kids, husbands, family members, friends, coworkers, a sweet lady at the checkout or at the bank, and to those in our sphere of influence. But we don't have to speak words we will regret.

Proverbs 25:11 in the *NET* says, "Like apples of gold in settings of silver, so is a word skillfully spoken."

I *love* the word "skillfully" in reference to the words we use. We can't speak words of wisdom unless we do so skillfully. Using the right words at the right time in the right circumstances is a powerful tool in the lives of our kids.

As moms, we can choose to be skillful with our words. Here's how to do this:

1. Pray. Take a second to get your mind right by consulting with your Creator before you say what's on your mind.

2. Think before you say one word, *What do I want to accomplish with my words?*
3. Ask yourself, *What will be the result of what I'm getting ready to say?*
4. Ask, *How can I most effectively help my child learn from this experience?*
5. Be careful to control your tone. It is not only what you say but also how you say it.
6. Don't yell. You're the parent and, contrary to popular belief, yelling does not work; it only shows you are losing control, and when you yell, you lose.
7. Make sure your response is equal to the offense or the circumstance. Don't overreact.
8. Choose to use words that will be building blocks to your kids' character and foundational to their faith.
9. Be realistic about your expectations and make sure your children have a clear understanding. It may just be that they didn't understand.
10. Give your kids grace. We all fail. We all make mistakes. And while it is very important that you teach your children right from wrong and that you discipline them when necessary, our kids can begin to discover God's grace through the grace you show them.

As moms, may we heed the lyrics to this sweet Sunday school song, "Oh, be careful little mouth what you say. Oh, be careful little mouth what you say. For the Father up above is looking down with love, so be careful little mouth what you say!"

The Father up above *is* looking down with love, and the little lives He has placed in our families are looking up for love, so speak words of wisdom, sweet mom. You are molding your child's life by the things you do and the words you say.

A Prayer for Mom

Precious Father, I know Your Word says that life and death are in the power of the tongue and knowing that can be a little scary!

Help me speak life into my children's lives and help me control my tongue so that I never wound my children's hearts with my words. Lord, I realize my children look to me to be their biggest encourager and to give them sound advice, so please help me never be callous, critical or cruel when I speak to them. And please help them grow up to be men and women who wield their words wisely and speak life instead of death.

More for Mom

Wielding Your Words Well

1. Have you ever observed a momma treat her child like the woman in the story at the beginning of this chapter?
2. Have you ever been the momma others have observed in the store?
3. What are some ways you can begin wielding words well with your kids today?

Lori's Story

4. How did Lori and her husband pour words of life into their little girl's life?
5. Do you think their daughter would have overcome her obstacles if her parents hadn't continually spoken very skillfully crafted words?
6. What words could you begin using to help your children overcome their obstacles?

Genny's Story

7. Genny was reminded of the power that is found in the simple things we say and the way we talk to our children. How does her story encourage you as a mom?
8. When you push the rewind button in your mind, what do you see when it comes to the way you speak to your children?
9. Why does what you say, as well as the way you say it, matter?

The Power of Our Words

10. What words have affected your life and the way you see yourself?

11. What healing needs to take place in your own life from words that have wounded your heart?
12. When you look at the verses that can help you think through your word choices before they come out of your mouth, which verse helps you most?

Practically Speaking

13. Have you ever been the recipient of negative word choices?
14. Have you ever said any of those to your children?
15. Which of the 10 helpful tips did you feel were most helpful and why?

7

CHARACTER COUNTS

For the Lord grants wisdom! From his mouth come knowledge and understanding. He grants a treasure of common sense to the honest. He is a shield to those who walk with integrity.
PROVERBS 2:6-7, *NLT*

With our morals currently being defined by shows like *Here Comes Honey Boo Boo* and *Pretty Little Liars*, it is becoming increasingly difficult to teach our kids what it means to live lives of moral character. Character is defined as the mental and moral qualities distinctive to an individual. It's something that is caught much more than it is taught. While friends may test the character of a child, it is the mother who molds it. "Character Counts" will highlight specific character traits and offer practical teaching tips. It will also emphasize the responsibility a mother has to be the kind of woman she hopes her children will be.

What Is Character Anyway?

On August 28, 1963, Martin Luther King, Jr. stood on the steps of the Lincoln Memorial and uttered these famous and historical words: "I have a dream that my four little children will one day live in a nation where they will not be judged by the color.of their skin, but by the content of their character."

Character is an interesting thing. It is who we really are. It defines us—or some might say, by it, we are defined. Recently, I was talking with a mother who was concerned about some of the things her son was doing. When she confronted him, he said, "Mom, we are not defined by the things we do." To which she replied, "What we do doesn't define us; it reflects who we already are." Character is defined as the attributes or features that make up an individual. Good or bad, our character is who we are and what we do reveals who we are.

In Matthew 12:35 (*NIV*), Jesus said, "A good man brings good things out of the good stored up in him, and an evil man brings evil things out of the evil stored up in him."

And in Proverbs 4:23 (*NIV*), we find this warning: "Above all else, guard your heart, for everything you do flows from it."

The things we do, the choices we make, the way we act and react flow from who we are and reflect the content of our character. In some ways, the things we do make us who we are. In other ways, the things we do reveal who we already are. It's basically a two-edged sword. Our character shapes our actions and our actions shape our character.

John Wooden once said, "Be more concerned with your character than your reputation, because your character is what you really are, while your reputation is merely what others think you are."

And who we are really matters. That's why character counts. But in a world where *Honey Boo Boo* rules and *Pretty Little Liars* are revered, how is a momma supposed to imprint godly character in the heart of her children? How can we counter this culture of shock radio and reality TV? How do we instill character traits like integrity, truth, honor and trust when the world in which we live in minimizes and even mocks them? How do we prevent disrespect at a time when respect for God, life and all things sacred is at an all time low? How do we fill our kids' hearts with a strong sense of morality when those with good morals are mocked and maligned?

Going against the cultural flow isn't easy when our children are constantly bombarded with bad behavior and told it is normal. But moms are given the purpose, position and power to plant seeds of character in the hearts of their children. Seeds that begin to sprout through those teachable moments where life lessons become the fertilizer that causes growth to occur. The fruit our children bear start with the seed their mommas sow.

Moms are heart-shapers who mold not only the hearts of their children but also the heart of the next generation. That's who you are, sweet mom! A world-changer. And those little hearts need you to be strong, bold, courageous, consistent and lead the way. It is by living a life of character that the character you long to see developed in your children is validated.

Genny's Story

As she drove her daughter, Katie, home from swim team one evening, Genny was weary and worn out. The whole day had been a battle and all she could think was, *Some days, parenting is hard!*

She couldn't remember what the issues were, but it seemed everything had been a challenge that day. Perhaps it was because they had a busy schedule and Genny had been impatient. Or maybe it was because Katie was almost 11 and becoming more independent. But whatever the reason, Genny was frustrated, Katie was mad and it was definitely one of those days.

As they drove home on the heels of an argument, Genny sighed, then Katie sighed. The silence was deafening and Genny could almost hear Katie cross her arms as she sat in the back seat, seething. Then Genny shifted mental gears and broke the ice with a much-needed conversation.

"You know what?" Genny said.

"What?" Katie answered as she sulked.

Genny continued, "I just realized, even when we have our differences, you and I are still more the same than we are different."

Katie remained silent.

"And I think the fact that we disagree sometimes might be good," Genny said as she did her best to use their frustration as a teachable moment.

Katie's heart and voice began to soften as she whispered, "Why?"

Genny drove home a very important point about character as she told Katie, "Because I see your determination. You have a strong will, and you can do a lot of great things with that in life."

Katie only responded with a quiet "Hmmm?" and then about five minutes later she broke her silence and somewhat shyly said, "Mommy . . . I love you."

Taken by surprise, Genny quickly replied, "I love you too."

Katie went on to thank her momma for taking her to swim team, and Genny's heart began to smile as she thought about how using that challenging moment as a teachable time was so much more effective than winning a battle of the wills.

Some days, parenting is hard, but even when it is, those are opportunities not only to intentionally speak words of wisdom, but also to embed character in the hearts of our children.

Genny shifted emotional gears and demonstrated the woman she wants her daughter to become. With a change in tone and a few wise words, Genny used a tense time between a mom and a preteen to convey the character of leadership into the heart of her strong-willed little girl.

You see, the strong-willed children of today are the adult leaders of tomorrow. But if parents don't help children channel their strong wills in the right direction, they won't bloom into leaders who lead with character and integrity. Instead, their potential may stagnate or they could become leaders who don't understand how to lead effectively.

As mommas, we know life can be hard and parenting is not for sissies. But it is often in those moments when parenting is off-the-charts difficult that we are given the most opportune time to coach our kids' character.

That's exactly what Genny did when she and Katie were at their wits' end. Genny turned what could have been a bad argument and a very long ride home into a sweet time between a mother and daughter and a character-building block that would be tucked in her daughter's heart for the rest of her life.

Rebekah's Motherhood Mess-up

In chapter 5 ("May I Have Your Attention?"), Rebekah taught us much about what can happen when we give too much attention to one child. But as we pull back another layer of this story, we will discover that Rebekah also teaches us a lot about how our own character affects the characters of our kids.

Remember the story. Rebekah was a wife who probably found herself feeling as barren as her womb. She and Isaac had been married for 20 years and they didn't have any children (see Gen. 25:20,26). In a time when a barren woman was ostracized and even thought to be forsaken by God,[1] Rebekah was likely desperate for a tiny tot to fill her arms, her time and her heart and to give her husband a child. While mothers around her had children tugging at their tunics, Rebekah probably longed for the day when the same would be true for her.

After seeking his Father's face on behalf of his barren wife, Isaac soon discovered that his prayers had been answered. Rebekah was carrying not just one but two babies in her womb and they were soon to be the proud parents of twins.

She may have had a maternal glow on her face, but there was a war going on in her womb that was destined to last a lifetime. Two boys longed to take the lead. One was chosen. One was not.

As I shared in chapter 5 ("May I Have Your Attention?"), childbirth for Rebekah only served to prove that all that wrestling in her womb was real. Those twins never seemed to abandon their race for first place, and the fact that Isaac and Rebekah played favorites only intensified the boys' fight to be number one. As parents, Isaac and Rebekah had the opportunity to mold the characters of their kids, but rather than helping their children embrace their own God-given identities, Rebekah became a meddling mom and Isaac continued to be a disengaged dad when it came to Jacob.

When Esau sold his firstborn birthright for a pot of stew to his ever-conniving and character-flawed brother, Jacob, he gave up the right of the firstborn. But when Daddy Isaac decided to divvy out the blessings of the firstborn, he either wasn't aware or perhaps he didn't care that Esau preferred a full belly to his birthright.

Rebekah, however, wanted to help her beloved boy, Jacob, wiggle his way to the front of the line. So she created a scheme to ensure that Jacob would receive the blessings of the firstborn:

> But Rebekah overheard what Isaac had said to his son Esau. So when Esau left to hunt for the wild game, she said to her son Jacob, "Listen. I overheard your father say to Esau, 'Bring me some wild game and prepare me a delicious meal. Then I will bless you in the Lord's presence before I die.' Now, my son, listen to me. Do exactly as I tell you.

Go out to the flocks, and bring me two fine young goats. I'll use them to prepare your father's favorite dish. Then take the food to your father so he can eat it and bless you before he dies" (Gen. 27:5-10, *NLT*).

When Jacob questioned his mischievous momma, she sealed her sneaky deal with words she would live to regret:

And Jacob said to Rebekah his mother, "Look, Esau my brother is a hairy man, and I am a smooth-skinned man. Perhaps my father will feel me, and I shall seem to be a deceiver to him; and I shall bring a curse on myself and not a blessing." But his mother said to him, "Let your curse be on me, my son; only obey my voice, and go, get them for me" (Gen. 27:11-12, *NLT*).

And so it was. The curse was on her. In her efforts to gain the blessings of the firstborn for her favorite son, she not only caused him to lose any sense of character he had, but she also lost the joy of ever seeing him again.

It's so easy to try to manipulate our kids' circumstances, to attempt to hold on to their futures and guide their destinies in the way we think they should go, rather than the way God wants them to go. It's hard for a momma to let her children experience pain, problems, consequences and chaos. But our children need to experience how God works in their lives on their own. The God who is real to us must be real to them, and we mommas need to get out of the way so that God can be God in their lives.

In order for them to know the Savior, they must first see themselves as sinners in need of one. In order for them to know God the Father, they must first feel the need for a father. In order for them to desire to be set free, they must first understand they are enslaved. In order for them to walk by faith, they must first discover how empty it is to walk by sight. In order for them to trust God's promises to be true, they must first seek His face for themselves.

In Genesis 25:23, God told Rebekah that the older would serve the younger. It was a prophetic promise for her boys. Regardless of the fact that Jacob was the second born, he would ultimately rule over his elder brother, Esau. But Rebekah's feeble faith prevented Jacob from discovering how God fulfills His promises to His people when they choose to wait on Him.

Many moms get in the way of what God wants to do in their children's lives because they're too busy trying to cushion their kids' consequences or defining their destinies. God reveals Himself in the trials, troubles and transitions of life. Character is often created in the crunches of life, when our response to life's struggles reveals who we really are and what we need to work on to become a better person.

Faith is often forged in the midst of our fear and failures. It is in response to the times when the unknown beckons us to believe there has to be a God because we realize that without Him life is pointless

Rebekah somehow forgot that Jacob's faith and character would be compromised by her deceitful and domineering decision to push Jacob to the front of the firstborn blessing line.

Erin's Story

Erin's children were at the age when they were expected to help around the house. They each had their rooms to clean and other chores to do throughout the week. It was a big blessing to have little hands helping around the house and Erin knew she was also preparing them for real-life expectations and responsibilities.

As adults these children will have jobs, homes, bosses, church leaders and a mile long to-do list of the things they will need to take care of around the house and in life. Erin wanted to intentionally prepare her kids for what she knew would come their way.

But, as with most children, when they grew older, Erin's kids began to roll their eyes and resist their momma's requests when it came time to divvy out their duties. They figured out that if they could make mom feel guilty about giving them a list of things to do, then they could win that war and enjoy some comfy couch time in front of the TV, hanging out with their friends or playing with the latest app on their smart phones. (And I can't believe kids actually have smart phones! Just sayin'!)

Unfortunately, Erin's kids succeeded in creating doubt in her heart and made her feel terrible about giving them chores. They mastered the art of making excuses, devising distractions, and pretending to actually want to do their homework. They knew that if they could make momma show them how to fold the towels the right way again, she just might end up doing them herself.

They were well aware that if she had to deal with their attitudes or explain to them how to clean the kitchen correctly one more time, she might get so weary and worn out with it all, or so frustrated by their endless arguing, that she would give in, let them get their way and do it herself. Or better yet, they could completely win the war and make her feel guilty about requiring them to help around the house. If they did that, then she might not divvy out the daily duties anymore.

It's never easy to feel like the bad guy when you're a good mom who is helping her children become the adults they were created to be: faithful, honest, compassionate, humble, hard-working, dependable, godly men and women of integrity who love God and live for Him and who make a difference in their generation. But those traits don't trickle into our hearts by osmosis. They are born and bred through challenges we face, commitments we make and examples we are given.

If you want to teach your children to be faithful, give them opportunities to be faithful. Give them room to fail, room to grow and room to try again. Teach them why faithfulness is such an important character trait. Point out faithfulness in their lives and in the lives of others when you see it. Help them see the problems and pitfalls that come with being unfaithful.

Moms help build integrity in the hearts of their kids one block at a time. It's in those moments when our circumstances are hard, the pressure is on and we feel weary, worn out and overwhelmed that our lives will speak louder than words as to what integrity looks like in real life.

Humility is born when our pride is threatened and our reputations are on the line. That's when we can show our children what humility looks like. When our fear is big and our faith is small, we are presented the privilege of giving our kids a bird's eye view of how mustard-seed-sized faith can overcome a mountain of fear.

The Character of Biblical Characters

My boys are men now, and throughout the years, they have been the object of my prayers. Kids have a way of consuming a momma's prayer life and mine are no different. I wish I would have known then what I know now about praying Scripture for my kids. Oh, I prayed God's Word for my sons, but over the years those prayers have changed. I realized that my prayers for my children should be as intentional as my parenting needs to be and so must yours.

We must be praying not only for their salvation and for their future spouses, but also praying that God will make them men like David, who had a heart after God; like Moses, who was humble, yet courageous; like Samuel, who longed for the voice of God and boldly stood for what was right; like Ezra, who passionately pursued God's Word and God's will; like Nehemiah, who united and protected God's people and who courageously fulfilled God's call in spite of persistent opposition. Men like Paul, who relentlessly led the way and laid the groundwork for the early church. Men like Peter, who fessed up when he messed up; and although he wasn't perfect, he was passionate about Christ and making a difference in his generation. Men like Peter and David, whose examples teach our kids that failure is never final; and like Solomon, who reminds us that wisdom does not equal perfection.

We need to pray that our kids will be men and women of character—the character of courage and tenacity demonstrated by Esther and Abigail. The character of loyalty and leadership as Ruth and Deborah had.

We will talk about this more in chapter 12, but consider using the character traits of biblical characters to pray for those attributes to be made real in your children's lives. Your kids will grow up and face challenges that will not only try their character but also test their faith. You have a few precious years to instill in them that which no one else will be able to shake.

You can instill character into your children by using real-life circumstances as teachable moments. You can teach them to think things through on their own by not giving them the answers for every situation. You can teach them by allowing them the wisdom that comes from making wrong choices and by allowing them to fail and discover the consequences and lessons that can only come from what happens when we don't choose well. And most of all, you can do that through demonstrating in your own life the type of character you want to see growing in them.

Sweet momma, you are not only molding the hearts of your precious children; you are also molding the hearts of the next generation. The things you say and do will be etched in their hearts for as long as they live. So with each new day, ask the Lord to help you live intentionally and parent intentionally. Ask Him to make the content of your character such that it will create a longing in their hearts to become people of God—just like their momma.

A Prayer for Mom

Lord, it's so hard to instill character in my kids when we live in a world where Honey Boo Boo and Pretty Little Liars seem to set the cultural standards. Please give me the wisdom to convey character by the way I live my life in front of my children, to be the kind of person I want them to grow up to be. Help me not be wishy-washy when it comes to teaching them about moral absolutes, integrity, honesty, loyalty, purity, kindness, humility and responsibility. I know it's not going to be easy, so I'm asking You to lead me, to protect my children from the lies of this world, to give them the discernment to distinguish between right and wrong, and to give them the courage to stand in the face of moral opposition. Help them go against the flow when their convictions and character are compromised by the culture.

More for Mom

What Is Character Anyway?
1. What is character?
2. Do you agree with this quote: "What we do doesn't define us; it reflects who we already are"?
3. Why is character so important?

Genny's Story
4. What are some character traits Genny may have helped her daughter develop by the way she handled their argument?

5. How did Genny's way of dealing with the situation demonstrate intentional parenting?
6. Do you struggle with putting your own emotions aside when parenting your children?

Rebekah's Motherhood Mess-up
7. How did Rebekah's love for her son and desire for him to succeed create some major character flaws in his heart?
8. What could she have done differently?

Erin's Story
9. Why is it important for kids to learn to be responsible?
10. Erin's kids succeeded in making her doubt that what she was doing as their parent was right. They even tried to make her feel guilty. Why is it that parents sometimes feel guilty when training their children to become responsible adults, and how can you win the battle of the wills when it comes to teaching your children character?

The Character of Biblical Characters
11. How can you use biblical characters as a way to teach character to your kids?
12. What are some character traits you would like to work on in your own life so that you can be a good example to your children?
13. What are some character traits you feel you need to work on in your kids?

Note
1. Albert Barnes, *Notes on the Bible*, Internet Sacred Texts Archive, 1834. http://biblehub.com/commentaries/isaiah/54-1.htm (accessed March 2014).

8

OVERWHELMED

From the end of the earth I call to you when my heart is faint.
Lead me to the rock that is higher than I.
PSALM 61:2, *ESV*

How ironic! We live in a world with tons of gadgets designed to make our lives easier, yet the only thing that seems to come easily is the tendency to feel overwhelmed. Life can be daunting, and being a mom isn't easy. It's hard to deal with the dailies of mommy-hood when you're trying to be all and do all and finding yourself overwhelmed by it all. Motherhood is messy, but it can be the most beautiful mess you ever imagined. Discover joy in your messy mom journey. Escape the pressures of being a perfect parent or trying to be like other moms. Embrace the reality that you're not in this mom thing alone.

What's the Big Deal?

Overwhelmed. It's where most moms live. Somewhere between the mounting piles of laundry, the unexpected flat tire, doctors' appointments, soccer practice and the pot of spaghetti boiling over on the stove, there is a mom who is at her wits' end. Perhaps that's you, sweet mom—wishing the load was lighter yet knowing you wouldn't change it for the world.

Being a mom means your days are full, you're always on the move and you've worn yourself out trying to juggle it all. The solution to your weary and worn-out heart can be as simple as just saying no. Becoming a mom who is strategic with what she agrees to do can really help lighten her load.

Overwhelmed comes in all shapes and sizes and for a multitude of reasons. It's not always because of our crazy busy days and never-ending to-do lists. Sometimes, it's in the silent moments when we mull over the way we mother or the voices in our hearts that cry out, *You're not enough!* And then there are those times when we feel overwhelmed, but for some reason, no one else is feeling the pressure and that just makes it worse.

One day, while packing for vacation, I found myself feeling very overwhelmed. My husband was working late and I felt the entire responsibility was on me to get things ready so we could pull out of the driveway at 4:30 AM. I never figured out why my man thought before the crack of dawn was a good time to wake up two young boys and begin our seven-hour jaunt to the mountains, but he was a man on a mission and we had a schedule to keep.

I tried really hard to make sure everything was all packed and ready to go, but every time I put something in the suitcase, my eight-year-old would take it out. Every time I tried to pack the snacks, my boys thought I put them on the table for a treat. Those fellas had a special talent for undoing everything I did, and after repacking their clothes for about the fifth time, I was about ready to throw a hissy fit. (Ever thrown one of those? If you have, you know it's not a pretty sight.)

And then there was the cleaning. I'm not sure why I thought the house had to be meticulous before we put the car in reverse and made our way to our mountain paradise, but I did. Maybe it was because if it wasn't spic and span and something happened to us, I was afraid someone would come in and discover how we really live. Unfortunately, my quest for clean became the straw that broke the camel's back and that hissy fit I was talking about became a reality.

Why can't you just play in your rooms until I get everything ready?

What in the world are you thinking? You know you're not allowed to have three Little Debbie Snacks for dessert!

Can't you see that I'm trying to get ready for our trip? Why can't you two help your momma instead of making things so difficult?

And, of course, that was a very mild look at my meltdown. Imagine a momma with a frazzled-looking face, a furrowed brow, and a voice somewhere between yelling and crying. Yeah . . . that was me.

The thing is, packing for our annual vacation was nothing new. I had mastered the mayhem of suitcases, coolers, cleaning and kids before. But for some reason, this year was different. I was overwhelmed by my own expectations.

I wanted my two boys to see that their momma needed help and begin to pitch in. I wanted to have everything done and them in bed by 9:00 PM. I didn't want to have to pry my kids out of bed before the break of day in order to leave in the cover of darkness. And I certainly didn't want to clean up behind my kids when I was trying to clean my house.

I had a lot of expectations going on in my mind—things that all could have been worked on and worked out. But because I was too busy fussing and fretting, I missed out on some teachable moments and a lot of laughter with my kids. I could have used those moments and taught them to think beyond themselves and discover the joy of helping others. Those moments could have been a time when we laughed together as we planned the great adventures we were going to have during the days to come. I could have made cleaning fun during those moments or helped them earn a few extra dollars for the trip and taught them the benefits of working hard for what you get. Instead, I made a big deal out of a lot of little deals and made what could have been a fun night with the kiddos become a night I hoped they would forget.

So, what was the big deal?

Really, there was nothing earth shattering going on. Just a whole lot of little things that wouldn't even reach a 1 on the Richter scale. Just the right mixture of attitude, expectations and maybe even hormones has the potential to reach seismic proportions.

Sometimes those big deals aren't so big after all. But it's the culmination of the seemingly insignificant that often spirals our emotions out of control and we find ourselves responding to the circumstances of life rather than parenting on purpose.

When the beans boil over, the light bulb goes out, your two-year-old is tugging on your trousers and someone is knocking at the door, it's a recipe for a meltdown moment. When you're running late for your son's soccer game, you can't find your keys, and your eight-month-old throws up on your brand new blouse as you're on your way out the door—that might just make a momma want to sit down and cry. None of these is a big deal by itself. But somehow those little mole hills become mountains when mounted on top of one another, and overwhelmed is bound to happen.

We don't always handle life as we should. A mom's life is full of little mishaps, messed-up plans, missed events and mistakes. As I packed our bags for a memory-making vacation, my emotions ran high and my attitude hit an all-time low. I learned some very valuable lessons that night. I learned that my emotions don't always have to win. I don't always have to react to the moment, and I can overcome being overwhelmed when I stop, pray and put everything into perspective.

I made a big deal out of what was going on that night, when there were no really big deals—only little ones that I gave far too much credit to. The next time you feel overwhelmed, stop, pray and put everything into perspective by asking yourself, "What's the big deal?"

Pressure to Be the Perfect Parent

Mirror, mirror, on the wall, who's the best mother of all? Okay, so who's almost the best? Well, maybe not almost the best, but am I at least a bit better than adequate?

Parenting was way different than I imagined it was going to be, and not long after I had my first son, I found myself wondering what in the world I was doing—longing to be the perfect parent and knowing I wasn't anywhere close. I'm not sure why, but before I had kids I thought being a mom would be easy. Even after my son was born, I was deluded into thinking I had the mom thing down. Maybe it was because at 18 I was way too young and immature to see beyond the soft, cute, cuddly baby boy in my arms. Perhaps it was foolishness, arrogance, or maybe just naivety, but I really thought parenting was going to be a breeze and I was somehow going to automatically become the perfect parent.

After all, the dreams of motherhood dancing in my head had me sporting a Super Mom costume, adorning my home with treasured homemade trinkets created by my kids, baking chocolate chip cookies and raising two sons who loved Jesus with all their hearts and who would boldly proclaim Him to the world. I had built a wall of expectations for myself as a mother, but all I was really doing was setting myself up for failure, and I didn't even realize it.

I had planned to be the mom who never yelled at her kids—the one who always kept her cool, who knew how to shepherd her children's hearts, and whose kids were never disobedient. Failure number one. I was going to be the mom who planned out every day, kept her kids on a strict schedule, always fed them healthy food, and never missed any of her children's activities. Failure number two. I had visions of creating the perfect family dinners in my perfectly organized home, where mismatched socks were nonexistent, and the spices stayed in alphabetical order. Failure number three. I thought we would have the perfect family vacations (I know—I blew that one big time!), and that we would have weekly game nights and family field trips to the park, the zoo and the beach. Failure number four.

Oh, there were a lot more failures to my perfect parenting dreams where those came from, but reflecting on how skewed my real view of motherhood was is pretty tough on my momma heart. Let's just say it didn't take long for me to discover that imperfect people can't be perfect parents. And there is no such thing as perfection when imperfect parents raise imperfect little people.

What I thought would make me a strong momma only proved to make me weak, and my own expectations of being the perfect parent left me feeling like a failure. I didn't measure up to my own illusion of mommy-hood. And I also didn't measure up to anyone else's either.

Every parenting book I read, every video I watched, and every conference I attended always made me feel like I could conquer the perfect parenting thing once and for all. Yes! I can do it! That is until I walked in the door of my house and discovered my eight-year-old had been hiding his report card because he had a bad grade; my eight-month-old was chewing up the cockroach he found in the corner of the sliding glass door; and I had forgotten to turn on the crockpot that morning before I left the house. Then, somehow, all those lessons I learned would get lost in the messiness of real life.

It's not as though the pressure I put on myself and the pressure I felt from parenting books, videos and conferences wasn't enough. No. The pressure that comes from living in the shadow of the seemingly perfect parents can leave a momma like me feeling overwhelmed and inadequate. The perfect parent never grows weary of playing tea with her two-year-old, racing cars with her little guy, creating crafts for her kids to do, or playing Hide-and-Seek for hours on end.

But I did.

The perfect parent isn't frustrated by the inconvenience of potty training, the distraction of a million and one questions, or the tactics kids use to get out of doing their homework.

But I was.

The elusive image of the perfect parent is just a notion we make up in our minds—a notion that comes from our own unrealistic and whimsical expectations of ourselves. A notion that comes from the misconceptions or even the misrepresentations in the books we read, videos we watch, and conferences we attend—a notion that comes from those seemingly perfect mommas who secretly and silently struggle with the same things every other momma struggles with.

Every attempt to chase the dream of perfect parenting has left this momma feeling very overwhelmed. Weary and worn out from trying to be something that was out of my reach, I finally discovered the freedom of knowing there are no perfect moms. Only moms like me and moms like you who love our kids like crazy, who fail our families daily, and who strive to be the best moms we can possibly be without being weighed down with the pressure to be the perfect parent.

There's so much joy and peace in knowing that you don't have to try to measure up. Don't let the quest to become a perfect parent overwhelm you and steal your joy. Perfect parenthood is not attainable. Never has been. Never will be. As Jill Churchill once said, "There's no way to be a perfect mother and a million ways to be a good one."

No Cookie-Cutter Kids

When my children were young, I saturated my mind with well-written parenting books designed to help readers become the best moms they could possibly be. Some held priceless parenting principles that are still etched on my heart today. Others overwhelmed me with charts, formulas and ten steps to becoming a successful mother whose children will turn out well—and that's a guarantee . . . well, almost.

Okay, so the books didn't come with written guarantees, but somewhere between the charts, the graphs and the carefully crafted words was the promise that if you followed their plan, your children would grow up to be faithful followers of the Lord Jesus Christ, and who live impressive and successful lives.

There really are no cookie-cutter children, no cookie-cutter parents, no cookie-cutter families and no cookie-cutter formulas that work for everyone. Each child is as unique as our individual fingerprints. Sometimes we see what works for one family and we think it will work for ours. We desperately try to implement the way those people parent their kids by doing the same things with our own children. Surprised and discouraged when things don't go as planned, we wonder what we did wrong. Did we miss a step? Why does it work with their children but not with ours? Because one size doesn't fit all. That's as true for pants as it is for parenting.

It can be overwhelming when we try to fit our families into another family's mold. Sure there are certain universal parenting principles, but God didn't create cookie-cutter people, so what works for your children and in your family won't necessarily work for another family, and vice versa.

I remember when I was learning about first-time obedience. We were given instructions to require first-time obedience at all times. It sounded great, so I was on board and ready to get going on the whole first-time obedience thing. The only problem was implementing it.

Our sons were two very different boys. If you have more than one child, I bet your kids are too. So, you can imagine our dilemma when it came to discipline. Karl (my oldest) was tenderhearted, compliant and obedient. All I had to do was give him the look and he would obey.

DJ was a different story. He was also tenderhearted, but he was nothing like his brother. DJ was strong-willed, rambunctious, inquisitive and adventurous. We could get on to him for something and he'd be right back at it two seconds later.

How do you implement the same rules for very different kids? First-time obedience sounds great in a parenting class, but making it a reality in our home was going to look very different for each child. Oh, I'm still a fan of first-time obedience, but as we tried to put that parenting principle into action, we discovered that it wasn't as easy as it looked. After trial and error (*lots* of error), we also learned that there are certain principles that are good for just about every family, but the methodology used to implement them must be as unique as our children.

Principles are general and are something that a majority of people can, will and even should embrace. Methodology is individual, subjective and strategically specific based on the needs of each family.

Here are a couple of examples of the how principles can be universal while the methods we use to implement them will be very different:

PRINCIPLE: Honesty

METHODOLOGY: Take their toys away when they lie. Put them in time out when they lie. Have them memorize Scriptures that teach us to be honest. Reward them with a special treat when they tell the truth, especially when it is hard. Help them understand the consequences of lying. Put them on restriction when they lie. Make them confess their lie to the one they lied to. If they are older and they lie, take away their cell phone or deny the privilege of going off with their friends.

Honesty is something each of us wants to instill in our children and there are tons of ways to teach our kids the principle of honesty. Each child will respond differently to the methods we use. Children whose feelings are easily hurt and who readily obey may not need to be put on restriction if they lie. Taking a toy away for a couple of days might get their attention just fine.

Strong-willed children may need to be put on restriction, and they may even respond better to positive reinforcement, so rewarding them for telling the truth in hard situations might do more to teach them the principle of honesty than disciplining them for dishonesty.

PRINCIPLE: A Lifestyle of discipline

METHODOLOGY: Give children a written schedule for their day. Teach them to develop their own schedule. Give them daily chores. Put them in time out or on restriction when they don't do their chores. Make them do their chores and their sibling's chores when they cop an attitude about doing their own. Instill Scripture about the importance and benefits of a disciplined lifestyle. Read books about people who were disciplined and highlight how discipline played a huge role in their accomplishments. Watch movies about those who were disciplined and talk about what they accomplished.

There is no one way to teach the value of a disciplined lifestyle to our kids. Each child is very different, so what works for one won't work for another. What one child responds to, another will rebel against. Each family is unique and your parenting methods will be very different from those of other families.

It's easy to feel overwhelmed when we dare to compare ourselves with other moms and our kids with other kids. Just remember, there are no cookie-cutter kids and one-size parenting does not fit all.

The Bible tells us in 2 Corinthians 10:12 (*NIV*), "We do not dare to classify or compare ourselves with some who commend themselves. When they measure themselves by themselves and compare themselves with themselves, they are not wise."

We had a friend who, just like me, was the proud momma of two boys. Only her sons were so well behaved it made me wonder what in the world I was doing parenting anyway. My boys weren't quite so poised. They loved to laugh and play. They liked making noise and hated going shopping. They fussed, feuded and occasionally fought. They complained, cried and sometimes moaned and groaned when things didn't go their way.

When I compared myself with her, I didn't measure up. My mothering seemed to pale in comparison to her and other Pinterest-perfect moms. I wasn't crafty or creative. I didn't bake my own bread or make every meal from scratch. I didn't color-coordinate our clothes as I hung them in the closet and I was definitely not a decorating diva. Then one day I realized Proverbs 22:6 really speaks to the individuality of our children and how our kids were given the parents they have for a purpose: "Direct your children onto the right path, and when they are older, they will not leave it" (*NLT*).

Wow! The Lord placed our children in our lives for a purpose. They were uniquely created to be pieces that help complete our family puzzle. We were specifically and intentionally placed in each others' lives by the Creator of the Universe.

That was a light bulb moment for me! I wasn't the perfect parent, but I was the perfect parent for them.

Other moms wondered how I could listen to my youngest son play the drums and the guitar so loudly, but I honestly didn't even notice. They wondered why I provided my boy with an endless supply of art supplies and a computer he didn't really need. But I did notice that when I helped feed his talents, he became more talented. Today, he is a graphic designer who is also an extremely gifted singer/songwriter.

Some moms didn't understand why I let my oldest play every type of sport on the planet. But it was what he loved. It kept him busy and fed his talents. Today, he uses his affinity for sports to minister to kids every week at the church he attends.

As my children grew, I realized I didn't have to overwhelm myself with an incessant attempt to become some other mom I was comparing myself with. I didn't have to fit my life into some-one else's parenting formula. I definitely wasn't a perfect mom, and that was okay, because I finally realized that I was the perfect mom for my boys.

You are the perfect mom for your children too. You are not a cookie-cutter mom, but a beautiful and unique gift to those little lives God gave you; so don't let yourself be overwhelmed by trying to be some other mother. Just be the best mom you can be for your kids and for the glory of God.

You Are Enough—Or Are You?
The Beautiful Dichotomy

Tammy was in her late thirties when she gave birth to her first child. The moment they placed that baby boy in her arms her heart began to beat at warp speed. "Oh wow! I'm a mom! What am I supposed to do with this little guy? He's so tiny! I'm not ready for this! I'm not enough! I sure hope my hubby has a clue!"

Not long after they left the hospital, her son developed diaper rash. They had read books about raising babies and were ready to tackle that rash on their baby's bottom. Tammy opened the drawer where her brand new, freshly washed cloth diapers were neatly stacked, and she took one off the top of the pile. As she unfolded it and placed it on her bed, she realized she didn't have a clue what to do with that thing.

"Good grief! Are you kidding? How do you fold a baby diaper? Hey, Karl, do you know how to fold a cloth diaper?"

I've known Tammy since we were both three years old, so I really wish I could have been a fly on the wall for that one!

After waging war with that diaper and folding and unfolding it a million ways, they both sat there staring at each other with a blank expression on their faces. Karl felt bad that he didn't know how to fold a cloth diaper for his baby boy, maybe even a bit frustrated. But Tammy felt like a failure as a mother. "Why don't I know how to do something so simple? Every mom knows how to do that! What's wrong with me? I'm definitely not enough to be the mom I should be!"

Almost every mom on the planet feels she isn't enough at one time or another. Maybe a cloth diaper has kicked your butt too and you were left feeling inadequate. Maybe it was during a time when your child was sick and you panicked because you never felt so helpless in all your life. Perhaps it was when the doctor walked into the room and told you your child has autism or some type of learning disability.

We've all been there. Feeling like we weren't enough, but knowing we had to keep being the mom. Maybe you're feeling like that right now: feeling inadequate, less than, not enough. I've been there too.

In fact, I actually lived there for far too long until I finally discovered the powerful truth. I am enough, but I'm really not.

It's a beautiful dichotomy that empowers a momma's heart like little else can.

I'm not mom enough. Never have been. Never will be. I don't have every answer to every situation they will face. I don't know the needs of their hearts and the way they should go. I'm not enough.

But I know the One who is. His name is Jesus—and He is always enough. Always has been. Always will be.

- He is enough when your son runs into the corner of the doorway and gives himself a concussion.
- He is enough when you get a phone call from a friend who is a single mom with three little ones who depend on her and she tells you that her heart condition is terminal and she only has about three months to live.
- He is enough when the thought of playing Hello Kitty Pop 'n' Play game one more time makes you want to cry.
- He is enough when the car breaks down, the washing machine is on the blink, and your toddler throws up while you're waiting in line at the bank.
- He is enough when money is tight, the rent is due, and you haven't even been to the grocery store yet.
- He's the same One who was enough to feed 5,000 with two fish and five loaves.
- He's the same One who was enough to give sight to the blind and life to the dead.
- He is the same One who was enough to lead His people out of bondage and then across the sea on dry ground.
- He is the same One who caused the winds and the waves to obey Him, healed the broken hearted, and comforted hurting hearts.

It's not a question as to whether I'm enough or not. The question is, do I trust the One who is? Because when I do, I become enough.

"My grace is sufficient for you, for my power is made perfect in weakness." Therefore I will boast all the more gladly of my

weaknesses, so that the power of Christ may rest upon me
(2 Cor. 12:9, *ESV*).

I don't have to be overwhelmed by my feelings of inadequacy.
There's power in knowing that knowing the One who is enough
makes me enough of a mom to be the perfect parent for my kids.
It's a beautiful dichotomy.

I can't do it. But I know the One who can.

I don't understand it. But I know the One who does.

I'm not wise enough to figure that out. But I know the One
who is.

I'm not enough. Perhaps I was never meant to be enough.
My inadequacies make me run and cling to the One who has no
inadequacies. I'm frail and fallible and in desperate need of the
One who is strong and infallible.

My children don't need me to be the perfect mom; they need
to see that I need a perfect God.

Sweet momma, don't be overwhelmed by feeling as if you have
to be enough. You only need to know the One who is enough, and
knowing Him, well, that makes you enough. You're mom enough
because He has made you mom enough. Enough to be a daughter
of the King, perfect and pure in His sight, a joint-heir with Jesus
Christ, forgiven, rescued, redeemed. He has given you all the things
that you need to live a godly life and He has equipped you for all
He has called you to, including mommy-hood.

We don't have to be overwhelmed anymore. We can press into
the One who says, "Take my yoke upon you, and learn from me, for
I am gentle and lowly in heart, and you will find rest for your souls"
(Matt. 11:29, *ESV*).

A Prayer for Mom

*Oh Lord, it's so easy to find myself drowning in the sea of mother-
hood. There's so much to do, so many expectations, and so many
ways I feel I just don't measure up. Help me embrace each messy
moment that comes my way as treasured time and teachable moments. Enable me to see past the sea problems we face every day,
not to compare myself with others, not to be deflated by my own*

*inadequacies, not to be overwhelmed by overwhelming circum-
stances, and to trust You to be enough and to make me enough
because I am Yours. Your Word says that I am complete in You, that
I have everything I need to live a godly life (see 2 Pet. 1:3), and that
You have made me more than a conqueror (see Rom. 8:37). Help
me live daily in that truth and not be an overwhelmed momma!*

More for Mom ❀

What's the Big Deal?

1. What are some things you need to say no to in order to be more strategic with your time?
2. What are some of the things that become big deals to you?
3. What are some ways you can prevent being overwhelmed by the big deals, the little deals, and everything in between?

Pressure to Be the Perfect Parent

4. Do you ever struggle with trying to be the perfect parent but feeling you can't measure up?
5. What books, videos or other moms have made you feel like you can't be the perfect parent?
6. What expectations do you place on yourself to be the perfect parent who always has her act together and always has the right answers?

No Cookie-Cutter Kids

7. Do you ever feel you need to be like another mother or that your kids need to be like other kids?
8. Have you ever thought that if you would do some type of 10-step program or follow some chart or graph, then maybe you could get the mom thing down?
9. How does understanding the difference between principle and methodology help you break free from the idea that one-size parenting fits all and help you not feel overwhelmed?

You Are Enough—Or Are You? The Beautiful Dichotomy

10. Have you ever wondered if you were enough or struggled with the idea that you weren't?

11. How does the truth that you're not enough but you know the One who is help you in your mom journey?
12. Jesus says that when we are weak, His strength is made perfect in us. How does that help you as a mom today? How can that keep you from feeling overwhelmed?

9

SETTING GOALS

But you, take courage! Do not let your hands be weak,
for your work shall be rewarded.
2 CHRONICLES 15:7, *ESV*

Have you ever wondered why we set goals for everything but parenting? If our goal for our children is that they grow up to love God, be good and godly spouses, caring and compassionate people and diligent workers, then wouldn't it be wise for us to chart a course in that direction and work on specific goals? There is no greater endeavor than that of molding the heart of a child. But how does a mother know if she is making progress in her attempts to cultivate her child's heart? "Setting Goals" will not only help mothers discern the effectiveness of their parenting in four key areas of their lives—spiritually, emotionally, educationally and relationally—but it will also help moms teach their kids how to set goals for themselves.

The Back Seat

My workload was piling up so I slipped into the back seat of the car and buried my head in my laptop. We were on our way to a family wedding, but I didn't have a clue where we were, and to be honest, I didn't care. I knew we were headed south. My hubby was behind the wheel and I was confident that we would eventually get there. I just didn't know how.

Arriving at an ultimate destination without knowing where you were going may work in the back seat of a car with a well-advised driver behind the wheel, but when it comes to parenting your kids, you are the one behind the wheel and it's important not only to know where you are going but also to chart the best possible course to get there.

A random journey in hopes of a specific destination is sort of like playing pinball and hoping you can control each move, that the ball doesn't end up stuck and that it won't end up going down the drain.

Given the option, we wouldn't allow our parenting to be so erratic. But oftentimes, that's exactly how we raise our kids—randomly. We hope for an ultimate outcome, yet we have no specific strategy to get there.

But what if we plotted a pathway to a preferred future for our kids and for ourselves? What would it look like if we decided to be more intentional about the goals we set for our kids and for ourselves? What if we parented the adult we long for them to become rather than simply dealing with the behavior of the moment? Wouldn't that change the way we parent?

Someone once said, "If you shoot for nothing, you will hit it every time." Where there is no goal, there is little, if any, progress. Setting goals will help you connect the parenting dots on your way to raising the adults you long for your children to be spiritually, emotionally, educationally and relationally.

When I was teaching my son to read, I gave him his first real book. It was *My Side of the Mountain* by Jean Craighead George. It wasn't a big book, but to my seven-year-old son it looked ginormous! He kept saying, "How am I going to read that whole thing?"

Glancing at him, I smiled and whispered, "One page at a time." That's how we live our lives. We turn one page at a time—we live one day at a time—and we fulfill our goals the same way.

But how can we help our children set goals and fulfill them? What types of goals should they have? In order to make goals that are unique and practical for each child, let's divvy up the areas of need and approach them with some specific solutions as we remember that many of them will cross over into other areas.

For example, patience is both a spiritual need and an emotional response that also demonstrates self-control. So, many of your goals will sort of mesh together.

The Jesus Example

In Luke 2:52 (*NIV*), the Bible says, "Jesus grew in wisdom and stature, and in favor with God and man," and as parents, we have the privilege of helping our children do the same. Using this simple verse, let's discover some very practical ways to set doable goals for and with our kids, and be sure to include your children in the goal-making process.

Jesus grew in wisdom (spiritually, educationally, relationally). Because true wisdom comes from God, begin to set some goals by choosing a book of the Bible or a specific passage of Scripture to study with your children. Develop a reading list that will help sow seeds of wisdom into your children's hearts, and schedule special events and activities to expand your children's awareness of life and strengthen their ability to navigate the circumstances they are sure to face.

Jesus grew in stature (physically, emotionally). Stature not only reflects the height of a person, but their reputation as well. Set physical and emotional goals to help your children be strong, eat well, establish healthy lifestyle habits and have a biblical view of themselves. When you consistently instill a strong sense of wellbeing and self-worth in the heart of your children, you embed confidence in their DNA. They will begin to value themselves, and taking care of themselves will become part of who they are, not just what they do.

Jesus grew in favor with God (spiritually, emotionally). The most important relationship we can have in this life is the one we have with the Living God. When you plant seeds of the Word through study and memorization, you cultivate a perennial harvest of truth in your children's lives. When you teach your children to pray and to know the significance of faith, worship, repentance and discipline, they will see God actively at work in their lives and begin to treasure their relationship with the Lord.

Jesus grew in favor with man (emotionally, relationally). It's easy to live in a house of mirrors where all we can see at every turn is me, myself and I. Teaching our children to be intentionally attentive to the needs of others and to live a life of compassion and caring will definitely be going against the flow. Help your children discover the joy of serving others. Make time to help a neighbor in need, visit a nursing home, make a meal for a friend, clean an elderly person's home or work at a homeless shelter. Help your children become aware of the needs of others and make their lives about so much more than themselves.

Parenting on purpose seldom comes easily. Life has a way of clouding our view of the goals we make and the steps we know we need to take to get there. It's a daily dilemma that requires a lot of persistence, patience and planning. An easy way to set goals and also help your children learn to set goals is to use these four categories as a filter for the decisions you make and the goals you set.

Erin's Story

Every Monday, Erin's third-grade son brought home a small packet of homework that was due on Friday. The first page was a reading log where he was to write a small paragraph about one of the books on the list. The other pages were math worksheets.

Erin frequently forgot about helping him with his homework until Thursday night and then found herself making a mad dash to situate her son at the table, rummage through a drawer in search of a sharpened pencil, and rush their way through a week's worth of homework.

She discovered that every Thursday night the pressure was on, the whining began and the tears puddled up in his eyes because he was overwhelmed by the rush of it all. It was just too much for a little guy to handle.

Finally, Erin realized that although her son was a smart little guy, he didn't handle pressure any better than she did. His whining was a response to putting the homework off until the last minute.

Erin decided it was time to make some changes in her approach to her son's weekly homework schedule. She set some goals and began to help him with a daily dose of homework instead of trying to fit it all in, in one night.

Helping her son see light at the end of his homework tunnel was an important building block on his way to discovering that he is capable of doing more than he had previously imagined. Had she not set those goals and divvied them up in doable chunks, he would have felt defeated and perhaps even deemed himself inadequate or incapable.

Erin set a goal that dealt with the immediate need of her son's education. But as with the making of a beautiful tapestry, every time she set a goal for her son and every time he conquered it, his accomplishments wove their way into his character and his view of himself changed dramatically. No longer was he emotionally handicapped by feelings of inadequacy. Now he is a winner, not a whiner. And now he has the confidence to conquer his goals.

Goals have a way of doing that—giving us a sense of accomplishment and making us ready for the next challenge. Goals help us not to be afraid of tackling something bigger than we are. Goals are as good for children as they are for parents.

Following the Footprints of Goal Setters

Throughout Scripture we look at the lives of those whom God called to accomplish the impossible and to be faithful in the ordinary. They were men and women who believed God, believed in themselves and set goals to do what God was calling them to do.

- When Abraham sent his servant to find a wife for his son Isaac, he sent him out with a specific goal and the details necessary to achieve it.
- When Moses led the children out of Egypt, his goal was the Promised Land. The details may have been mapped out by God, but Moses had to listen and obey.
- When David went to war, he did so not only with a goal in mind, but also with a plan for how he could reach it.
- When Esther laid her life on the line to save the children of Israel, her goal was clear and her strategy was sure.
- On every missionary journey Paul made, he set his sights on a goal and mapped out a plan to make sure it happened.

Goals get people to the places in life they long to go. But as we look at the examples of those who have gone before us, we can't miss the fact that it was God who directed them in the way they should go. Goals for you and your children should always be made prayerfully and in light of Scripture. Goals can also be risky because they come with expectations, obstacles and a certain amount of accountability, but the potential is worth the risk. Sweet mom, goals are just as important for your kids as they are for you.

I love what Thomas Edison said after countless failed attempts to create the light bulb: "I have not failed. I've just found 10,000 ways that won't work." He went on to say that "Many of life's failures are people who did not realize how close they were to success when they gave up."

Julie's Story

Julie's daughter JoHanna seemed to be held captive by an irrational fear of separation. Julie couldn't even get five feet away without her precious four-year-old freaking out. Julie knew that even at the age of four, they had to help JoHanna see her need to trust her parents and, ultimately, to trust God. Julie wanted her daughter to discover the freedom from fear that comes with faith and prayer, so she began to diligently teach JoHanna to pray.

Julie and her husband sat with JoHanna on the porch and began to gently walk her through the stages of what happened during her cycle of fear and what that moment of panic felt like. Her precious little heart had a big desire to trust God, so they began with the simple goal to "pray instead of panic."

To help JoHanna reach her goal, they took pictures of what each trust step would look like. The pictures included her initial reaction, stopping to bow in prayer and lifting her head with a smile of trust. They created a book using the pictures and read it to her often so that she could have a visual illustration of what reaching her prayer goal would look like.

JoHanna's journey to freedom from fear did not come without challenges. Each day she acted out the necessary steps to reach her goal of being a little girl who prays instead of panics. New habits began to form as her parents helped her reach her goal.

Many years later, JoHanna is a confident young woman who knows how to turn to her Lord, ask for His help and step out boldly into the unknown. She has reached her goal of learning to overcome panic with prayer. The once-small girl with little courage has grown into a strong young adult with a bold heart.

Julie's wisdom in helping her four-year-old hurdle her fears changed the course of JoHanna's life. Her faith and her character were at stake during that battle with fear. Julie helped JoHanna conquer fear and discover the faithfulness of God, the love of her parents and the God-given courage tucked deep within her own heart. We don't know for sure, but I believe that if Julie had ignored, indulged or surrendered to her daughter's fears, JoHanna wouldn't be the fearless young woman she is today. JoHanna grew in wisdom and stature and in favor with God through that life-changing experience.

Sweet mom, your role in helping your children set goals is priceless. If you're like me, you might need a few examples to help you get the hang of what helping your children set goals looks like in real life.

So, here are four specific examples of how you can help your children set spiritual, physical, emotional and relational goals. Remember, they will mesh together like the example we see of Jesus in Luke 2:52—wisdom, stature, favor with God and favor with man. (And be sure to let your children have a voice in making goals for themselves as often as possible.)

1. Growing in wisdom and favor with God—spiritually, emotionally and relationally

    - *Area of need:* Biblical foundation
    - *Goal:* Learn the Ten Commandments.
    - *Journey:* Organize an age-appropriate daily schedule of learning one commandment at a time with a specific starting and ending date.
    - *Follow-through:* Put the list somewhere convenient and begin to check off each day until your reach the goal.

2. Growing in wisdom and in stature—spiritually, educationally and in reputation

   - *Area of need:* Reading level increased
   - *Goal:* Read four books during the summer.
   - *Journey:* With input from your children, choose age-appropriate, character and faith-building books and make a daily schedule with a specific starting and ending date for each book. Be sure to discuss the lessons tucked in the pages of each book.
   - *Follow-through:* Begin each day with the reading plan and be sure not only to discuss the lessons but also to enjoy the journey of discovery with each book you read together. Remember, leaders are readers, so their ability to read will also help them have a good reputation as a leader in the future.

3. Growing in wisdom and in stature—physically, emotionally and spiritually

   - *Area of need:* Be healthy.
   - *Goal:* Exercise three to five times a week and eat balanced meals.
   - *Journey:* Choose and schedule age-appropriate games and/or exercises. Life is busy, so choose do-able activities. Try different sports, dance or ballet. Make a healthy meal plan together and stock up on some nutritious snacks.
   - *Follow-through:* So much depends on discipline, so be like Nike and "Just do it!" Don't let the day slip away without getting in at least 15 minutes of some type of exercise. Play Hide-and-Seek, kickball, dodge ball or tag with the kiddos. Make eating well a way of life. Buy carrots, celery sticks and/or other fruits and vegetables and call them "Free" snacks. Wash them and place them in the fridge. Let your children know they can eat these snacks any time, but the snacks of

the less-healthy variety will only be eaten once or twice a week.

4. Growing in wisdom and in favor with man—relationally, emotionally and spiritually

- *Area of need:* Compassion for others
- *Goal:* Complete five summertime service projects.
- *Journey:* Your children can choose five age-appropriate projects they can help with: mow a neighbor's yard, clean a shut-in's home, take a meal to a sick friend, bake cookies for an elderly neighbor, visit a nursing home, help at a homeless shelter, collect food for the needy, babysit for a single mom or raise money for a mission trip.
- *Follow-through:* After investigating how to get involved in local homeless shelters and nursing homes and finding out the needs of family, friends and neighbors, make a schedule for the summer giving your children five ways to help. Be sure to let them get in on the decision. They may have a preference or know a friend who needs help. It's a beautiful thing when they discover how to have compassion for others.

Goals help us all become who we were created to be and you are a vital part of helping your children not only make goals for themselves but also discover the joy of achieving them. But let's be honest: Not all goals are achievable, are they? What do we do when our kids set goals they are unable to achieve?

What If They Can't Do It?

Sometimes we are unable to hit the mark no matter how long and hard we aim. At times, unforeseen circumstances crop up and even the best made plans become impossible. Is that failure? Sometimes it is and sometimes it's not. But even if it is, we have the opportunity to teach our kids that failure is never final.

Their goal may be to make the baseball team, but if they don't, they need to know that not getting on the team doesn't define them. Sometimes the most important lessons are learned when we don't realize a dream.

Some of the most successful people in history experienced some of the greatest failures:

Winston Churchill failed sixth grade and was defeated in every political race he ran in, but he kept pressing on and became the Prime Minister of Britain when he was 62 years old.

Colonel Sanders was rejected by more than 1,000 restaurants in his attempts to sell his famous chicken, but today his own restaurants are found all over the world.

Steven Spielberg failed to be accepted by the college of his dreams three times and after trying a different college, he dropped out and began directing movies.

Walt Disney was fired by a newspaper editor and was told he had no imagination and no good ideas. He had several business failures before the premiere of his first movie: *Snow White*—and the rest is history.

Oprah Winfrey was a reporter who was fired and told that she wasn't fit to be on screen. I think they were wrong. Don't you?

Teaching our children that failure doesn't define them is a huge building block to their success. Not every goal will be achieved because perhaps they weren't meant to go there or be that or do that thing. Humility, discipline, wisdom, perseverance, patience and prayer are birthed somewhere between setting a goal and trying to achieve it. Even if it is never attained, the character built and the friendships that are forged make it all worth the attempt of achieving it. And whether your children exceed their goals or never achieve them, they know you will be their biggest cheerleader every step of the way.

Before we close out this chapter, let me share five ways that you can help your children discover, set and achieve goals:

1. Help them look back and see areas of need. Does their room stay a mess? Do they struggle with patience, unkind words or bad attitudes? Do they start things they don't finish, do things half-heartedly or neglect to do what they should? Do they eat too much, talk too much or whine too much? Do they pray daily, read God's Word—or if they aren't old enough to read, do you read it to them every day? Do they serve others? Do they struggle with sharing, telling the truth or controlling their temper? Help them look at who they are and who they will become based on who they've been.

2. Equip them to set doable goals. As with adults, they will quickly fall under the weight of a goal bigger than themselves. Help them see that the outcome is possible if they make small goals on their way to fulfilling their ultimate goal. If it's a bad attitude or unkind words and their goal is to eliminate them from their behavior, start by setting a daily goal of maintaining a good attitude and refraining from unkind words. Then stretch that timeframe to three days, then a week. If it's an incessantly messy room, do the same. Every day they are victorious, they are successfully fulfilling their goals.

3. Teach them that failure is never final. We all fail. We've all been on a diet and, in a moment of weakness, devoured a handful of Oreos and a half-gallon of ice cream. But failing doesn't make us a failure; it strengthens us and teaches us how to persevere and how to have mercy on others when they fail.

4. Be their biggest cheerleader. Teaching our children to set goals and fulfill them is kind of like teaching them to ride a bike. We run with them, holding them along the way. When we see them doing it on their own, we let go. They may fall, but when they do, we help them get back on the bike, and we run with them again until they're ready. The goal isn't to run beside them the rest of their lives. The goal is to teach them to do it on their own and then stand back and watch them soar!

5. Celebrate their victories. Children need to know you're proud of them, but more than that, they need to learn what it's like to be proud of themselves. Not arrogant— but that feeling of accomplishment that comes with knowing they set their heart on doing something, worked hard, maybe even sacrificed, and did it! Your heart will melt and their heart will be strengthened every time they are able to say, "Look, Mom, I did it!"

Parenting is seldom easy, almost always messy and sometimes frustrating. But you are molding the hearts of those precious children who need you not only to believe in them but also to help them believe in themselves.

Remember, you are shooting for a target every day you parent whether you realize it or not. The only way you will ever accomplish what you hope to is if you do it on purpose.

Oh . . . and if you aim for nothing, sweet mom, you'll hit it every time.

A Prayer for Mom

Lord, I realize that setting goals for myself, our family and my children is a very important part of parenting. Help me take the driver's seat of goal setting for my children so that my parenting and their lives won't be random and haphazard. Help me set goals that will encourage and stretch them to grow in wisdom and stature and in favor with God and with man. Help me be consistent and intentional in not only setting goals but also in helping them learn to set goals for themselves. I realize that not every goal set will be a goal that is met, so when that happens, help them learn valuable lessons from each unmet goal and give me the right words to help my children understand that failure is never final. And through it all, help me instill in their hearts that Your will is the ultimate target for every goal they will ever set.

❁ More for Mom

The Back Seat
1. Do you sometimes feel that you're parenting from the back seat? You know you are going to end up somewhere, but you aren't sure how you're going to get there.
2. How can being in the driver's seat of your parenting journey change the way you parent and the way you map out your journey with and for your children?

The Jesus Example
3. What does it mean that Jesus grew in wisdom and stature and in favor with God and man?
4. How can that apply to the way you set goals with and for your children?

Erin's Story
5. How did Erin's lack of setting goals affect her son?
6. In what ways is Erin's son better off because she was wise enough to notice a problem and decided to set goals for both of them?
7. In what areas do you need to set goals with and for your children, spiritually, emotionally, physically and relationally?

Following the Footprints of Goal Setters
8. If prayer was an inherent part of the success of Abraham, Moses, David, Esther and Paul, how can you incorporate prayer into your goal-setting plans?

Julie's Story
9. What might have been the outcome of JoHanna's fears if Julie had not stepped in and set some tangible goals?
10. How can prayerfully setting goals for your child in a specific area of need right now help strengthen his/her faith, trust in God and trust in you as parents?

What If They Can't Do It?
11. Why is it important to learn how to fail well?

12. What can you teach your children right now that will help build their character as they try to achieve their goals?

10

IMPRINTS MOMS MAKE

They are to teach what is good, and so train the young women to love their husbands and children, to be self-controlled, pure, working at home, kind, and submissive to their own husbands, that the word of God may not be reviled.
TITUS 2:3-5, *ESV*

Moms leave their imprints on just about everything they touch—their husbands, their homes, their family, their friends, their projects, the events they are involved with, and most of all on their children's hearts. Using the Proverbs 31 woman as the model, "Imprints Moms Make" will help moms discover their own uniqueness and the power of their influence, as well as help them in five key areas where their imprint will be felt most.

Imprints on My Home

My mother-in-law leaves her imprint on everything in her home. Every picture on the wall is adorned with a little extra something that makes it uniquely hers. A little porcelain butterfly pinned to the bottom corner of the picture hanging in the living room. A lace ribbon streaming from the top corner of a picture in the hall. Every table is graced with a special little knickknack. Every potted plant is enhanced with something that whispers, "Louise has been here"—a cute little ladybug hatpin sticking up out of the dirt of her fern plant. A pretty little rooster perched with its feet dangling on the window ledge right above the kitchen sink. Even her food is prepared with a special dash of this and a distinct dash of that. And the flavor of each dish she makes is notably hers.

She leaves an unmistakable imprint on her home. She's not the only one. You do too. And as much as this domestically challenged momma hates to admit it, so do I.

My imprint isn't as elaborate as Louise's. I'm not a shopper. I don't like going into stores, so shopping for decorations for my home is on the bottom of my to-do list, and to be honest, I never get to it.

Call me a minimalist, but our house still looks like it did when we moved back from the mission field—a few pictures on the wall and very basic (more like bare bones) furniture adorn our home. I try to keep it tidy, but decorating is definitely not a priority to me.

We're all different and God created us with very individual bents. Some women are into shopping, decorating, preparing big meals, and serving those meals on beautifully adorned dining room tables. Others are more like me. They don't like to shop, they don't like to decorate, they aren't great cooks, and paper plates will do just fine. And then there are those women who are somewhere in between.

It doesn't matter where you land on a scale from 1 to 10 (1 representing the lowest interest and 10 representing the most), you leave your imprint on your home. When my children were younger, I thought more about those little things that made our home ours, but after moving 11 times in 2 years while we were on the mission field and then moving back to the states, I kind of lost my flair for decorating, experimenting with meals, and being the hostess with the mostest.

Let's face it, there's a lot more to caring for your home than pretty decorations and gourmet meals. There's that not so fun thing to talk about called housework. We're moms and housework is a daily dilemma for us all. Our homes get messy, dusty and disorganized. Our kids' clothes get dirty, our toilets need to be cleaned, and our floors get these little balls of dust, lint and dirt that gather together and somehow resemble some sort of domestic tumbleweed. We always have a never-ending supply of dirty dishes and laundry. So, as much as we don't want to tackle this topic, we really must.

Cleaning for me has been a roller-coaster ride. I've gone from "Please don't come into my house because I'm a slob and you won't be able to find the floor," to "Sure, come on in . . . you can eat off the floor if you'd like." I guess I'm either all in or all out, messy or immaculate; so, for me, finding a good, healthy balance has been quite the quest.

As we look at where moms leave imprints, we're going to scan Proverbs 31 and get a glimpse of the intimidating Mrs. P31. Every time I study Proverbs 31, I shake my head and think that there's no way this woman existed. In theory, she didn't. She was the epitome of womanhood described by a mother who was giving her son advice about what kind of woman to marry—the Wonder Woman of the Bible.

In reality, Mrs. P31's qualities are qualities we can all have. Maybe not all at the same time and maybe not to the extreme that Mrs. P31 had them, but let's not sell ourselves short. Mommas have more moxie than they give themselves credit for.

So, let's take a look at the incredible Mrs. P31's approach to housework:

> She gets up before dawn to prepare breakfast for her household and plan the day's work for her servant girls. She is energetic and strong, a hard worker. She has no fear of winter for her household, for everyone has warm clothes. She makes her own bedspreads. She dresses in fine linen and purple gowns. She carefully watches everything in her household and suffers nothing from laziness (Prov. 31:15,17,21-22,27, *NLT*).

Oh wow! She really is all that and a bag of chips, isn't she? But didn't she ever have a bad week? Or even a bad day?

When I was studying the Proverbs 31 woman, I realized that nowhere in this powerful passage of Scripture do you find that she *loved* her husband or that she *loved* her children. To be honest, I think it's assumed she did. Women tend to do what they do for others because they love them. Housework is no different and caring for the needs of our families is no different today than it was then. *Love* is the why behind the what.

Mrs. P31 lived in a home where help was just a bell ring away. Most of us don't have help like that at our disposal (I'd be the first one to sign up if we did!). If the toilet needs to be scrubbed, it's up to us. If the dishes or laundry need to be done, we are normally the ones who take care of that.

Ultimately, those little things you do to leave an imprint in your home—the decorating, the housework, the home-cooked meals—those are all a labor of love. For some, you get excited thinking about a clean house with pretty decorations and carefully planned meals. For others, you would much rather be doing a million other things. But for all of us, it's part of how we love the ones we love well, even when it's a sacrifice for us to do it. Perhaps even especially if it's a sacrifice to do it. There are a ton of great resources to help us figure out how to get organized, how to clean our homes, and how to make them more inviting, but it all starts with the heart. Why do we do what we do?

You can start with one room at a time. You can work from the ceiling to the floor. You can begin at your front door and make your way around the house. You can start with your closet, buy specially made boxes to help you get things organized. You can simplify, spring clean, enroll in a cooking class, enlist a friend to help you decorate.

All of those are great ideas to help you get started. The goal, however, is to start somewhere, because when you do, you show your family and friends (but especially your family) that you love them, that you care about their environment, that you want to create a place of peace—a place where they know they belong.

I know I'm not a domestic diva and I realize it's hard for me to think in terms of scented candles and homemade banana bread, but when I take the time to care for my home, I'm telling my family and the people who visit that they are welcome; they are treasured; they are loved.

My house won't look like Martha Stewart's, and my food definitely won't taste like hers, but I can make my home neat and organized (just don't look in the hall closet!) and comfy. I can make it a place where people can come and feel relaxed and as though they belong, because they do, especially my hubby and my kids.

So, why is it so important to think about the kind of imprint you are leaving on your home? Well, it's really the why behind that what. It's what keeps us doing what may not come easily: because we love.

Imprints on My Husband

My husband knows I love him. I haven't always been the perfect wife and I haven't always said and done the right thing. But he knows I love him and he knows he can trust me. Even during the difficult years of our marriage when I really didn't like him very much, he knew I loved him and he could trust me.

The Scottish minister George MacDonald once said, "To be trusted is a greater compliment than to be loved." Husbands need to know they can trust their wives. Not just to be faithful, but in every area of the lives they are living together. A woman's trustworthiness is like sweet perfume; it permeates everything about her.

Check out what we can learn about the imprint Mrs. P31 left on her hubby:

> The heart of her husband trusts in her, and he will have no lack of gain. She does him good, and not harm, all the days of her life. She seeks wool and flax, and works with willing hands. She rises while it is yet night and provides food for her household and portions for her maidens. She considers a field and buys it; with the fruit of her hands she plants a vineyard. Her husband is known in the gates when he sits among the elders of the land. She opens her mouth with wisdom, and the teaching of kindness is on her tongue. She looks well to the ways of her household and does not eat the bread of idleness. Her children rise up and call her blessed; her husband also, and he praises her (Prov. 31:11-13,15-16,23,26-28, *ESV*).

The bottom line is that her hubby trusted her because she was trustworthy. She was committed to doing him good, she willingly worked hard, she made sure her man's belly was full (a big deal for every man on the planet!). She was wise and frugal with their finances. She not only encouraged and supported him, but she did what she could to help promote him. She was wise with her words, she wasn't lazy and the reward for all she did was that her children and her husband rose up and called her blessed. They praised her. Not after she died, but while she was alive.

My husband is my biggest cheerleader. The day I got the call from my agent and she told me Regal Books had said yes, I text messaged my husband. I knew he was in a meeting, so I didn't want to disturb him, but as soon as he got the message he called me back. He was as excited as I was.

A sweet friend who was in the room where his meeting was being held later told me that when he came back into the room, he shared the good news with the church staff and told them how proud he was of me and how he knew this book would minister to the hearts of moms and give the Church the tools it needs to help the Body of Christ make mentoring missional. It's my prayer that it does! That's the heartbeat of this book. I can't tell you how much it meant to know my hubby believed in me and was saying really sweet things about me to others.

- Mrs. P31's man trusted his wife.
- He knew that she was for him and wanted what was best for him.
- He knew he didn't have to worry about his wife running up the credit card.
- He didn't have to worry about her saying bad things about him behind his back.
- He knew he could trust her to support him.
- He knew she saw their marriage as a partnership and she worked hard to help her man make ends meet and keep the house running well.

Recently I was talking to a young lady who was struggling in her marriage. Her husband worked 10 to 12 hours a day to support the family while she stayed home with their little girl. Her house was an absolute mess and her floors hadn't been cleaned in years (really . . . literally years). He normally had to make his own lunch before he went to work, and she rarely made dinner for the family.

I'm not sure what she did during the day, but when he came home, she constantly hounded him about making more money.

Marriage is a partnership. Husbands and wives work together so they can help each other and to keep the home running smoothly. Husbands need to be able to trust that their wives will do their part, and wives need to be able to trust that their hubbies will do their part.

If Mrs. P31 was busy running up the credit card, her husband wouldn't have trusted her. If Mrs. P31 was too busy gallivanting around town to take care of her home, her hubby and their children, he wouldn't have been able to trust her. If Mrs. P31 wasn't willing to get off her duff and put a meal together for her man and tidy up their home a bit, then he wouldn't have been able to say, "I know we're in this thing together and I can trust my wife to help make our house a home and our marriage strong."

I've heard people say that in a marriage, trust is everything. If a man can't trust his wife, it's like knocking the legs out from under the foundation of their marriage. The same is true if a wife can't trust her husband. Trust is the seed that feeds love. Marriage may survive when the embers of first love fizzle out, but when trust is destroyed, the marriage is on dangerous ground.

A wife leaves an imprint on her hubby's heart when he knows he can trust her. And when he trusts her, every chance he gets, he praises her.

Imprints on Others

Our families know us best. But those in our sphere of influence are also affected by our lives. We leave an imprint on the lives of those we spend time with. Whether it's a good imprint or a bad one is up to us.

The way we treat others, the way we act and react, and the way we make others feel all have a way of telling people who we are and who they are to us.

When we were on the mission field, we quickly learned that what John Maxwell says is true: "People don't care how much you know until they know how much you care." No matter how much we wanted to share the good news of the Gospel, we couldn't expect people to listen while their bellies were growling.

The incredible Mrs. P31 knew exactly how to care for others. She woke up before the crack of dawn to provide for her household. She was held in great respect by those with whom she did business. She carried herself with dignity and grace, and she willingly gave to those in need. Her words were kind and her heart was tender. And she left an imprint on the heart of everyone with whom she came in contact.

> She rises while it is yet night and provides food for her household and portions for her maidens. She considers a field and buys it; with the fruit of her hands she plants a vineyard. She dresses herself with strength and makes her arms strong. She opens her hand to the poor and reaches out her hands to the needy. Strength and dignity are her clothing, and she laughs at the time to come. She opens her mouth with wisdom, and the teaching of kindness is on her tongue (Prov. 31:15-17,20,25-26, *ESV*).

I want to be like that. A woman who loves others well. One who sees the needs of others and is willing to be inconvenienced for the sake of meeting those needs. A woman who carries herself with grace, strength, dignity and integrity. A woman who speaks life into the lives of others. A woman who is wise and kind and leaves an imprint on the hearts of everyone she meets. A good imprint that points people to Christ and leaves them saying, "So this is what love looks like for those who follow Christ."

Scripture doesn't let us look into this woman's friendships, but I can't help but wonder how many mornings she enjoyed a cup of coffee with a friend. How many evenings did she gather together with her girlfriends as they sat around the dining room table, laughing about things no one else understood? How often did she run to help a friend clean her house before company came?

Friends are an important part of life, especially the mom life. Who else will listen to us rant about how ungrateful our kids are and still want to hang out with us? Who else will laugh at our corny jokes and cry with us as we watch *The Notebook* for the umpteenth time? Who else will go with you to a dreaded doctor's appointment, or hang out with you all night on Black Friday when neither of you likes to shop.

Throughout my life, the Lord has blessed me beyond measure with several good, godly friends. Each one is different, yet all of them are a very important part of my life. Friends are powerful influences in our lives. They can encourage us to live as we know we ought and can challenge us to accomplish what we think we can't. But on the flip side, they are also capable of dragging us lower than we thought we'd ever go and doing things we thought we'd never do. That's why it's so important that we choose our friends wisely. We all need the kind of friend who can speak truth into our lives even when it hurts. Do you have a friend like that? Are you that kind of friend?

Those friends that I've been blessed to know throughout the years have all left an imprint on my heart. I hope I've left one on their hearts as well. Mrs. P31 left an imprint on everyone she came in contact with. So do we. Sometimes it's good just to think about the kind of imprint we're leaving.

Imprints on My Child's Heart

Her children rise up and call her blessed; her husband also, and he praises her (Prov. 31:28, *ESV*).

Everything we read about the incredible Mrs. P31 was what her children would have experienced. They would have witnessed the way their momma was willing to sacrifice to take care of the needs of others. They would have seen the little things she did in her home to make it warm and inviting. They would have known how she worked late at night, got up early, spent hours sewing special clothes for them, how she managed the finances well, ministered to the needs of the poor, and diligently did business to help bring in some extra income.

Every meal she made, every stitch she sewed, every real estate deal she closed, every seed she planted, every late night spent working, every wise and kind word, everything she did left an imprint of love and faithfulness on the hearts of her kids.

Today, little eyes are watching you. They see the way you care for them, the special things you do, even when you're weary, worn out and overwhelmed. If you're married, they see the way you love your husband, the way you care for him by the little things you do, the way he knows he can trust you. They watch the way you minister to those you know and those you don't know. Everything you do, every sacrifice you make, every time you help them or someone else, they see it and the imprint you leave is indelible.

It's not easy being a mom, but no matter how you're wired, no matter what you're good at and what you're not good at, you are leaving an imprint on your home, on your hubby, on the hearts of everyone you come in contact with, and especially on the hearts of your children.

And as for all those sleepless nights, for all those long days, for all that hard work, for everything you do, one day you will realize that your family rises up and calls you blessed—that they praise you all because you have left an unmistakable imprint on their hearts.

A Prayer for Mom

Lord, I know the things I do and say leave an imprint on my home, my husband, my children and on those around me, so please help me leave imprints that reflect You well. I know I can't always be on my game in every area and that I'll never be the incredible Mrs. P31, but please help the character traits that caused her husband and her children to rise up and call her blessed to be character traits that I exhibit as I leave my imprint on the hearts and lives of those I love. May the imprints that I make leave an impression of Your love and grace.

More for Mom

Imprints on My Home

1. What are some areas you struggle with in your home? Decorating? Cooking? Cleaning? Organizing?
2. How can you begin to tackle the heart of your housework issue today?

3. How does it help you to know the reason you make your home a haven for your family and friends?

Imprints on My Husband
4. Would you say your husband can trust you with every area of your life together? Your home? Your finances? Guarding his reputation?
5. The Scottish minister George MacDonald once said, "To be trusted is a greater compliment than to be loved." How do you think trust could be a greater compliment than being loved?
6. What are some things you can do today to leave an imprint on your hubby's heart?

Imprints on Others
7. What kind of imprint are you leaving on the hearts of those with whom you have contact? Those with whom you work? Those in your neighborhood?
8. Would others say you carry yourself with dignity and grace?
9. What are some ways that you show you care about others? What are some things you can start doing today that will help others in need?
10. Do you surround yourself with mom friends who can help you in your journey? What kind of imprint are you leaving on their hearts?

Imprints on My Child's Heart
11. What do your children see in your life that is leaving an imprint?
12. What would you change if you realized your children were watching you?
13. What kind of imprint do you want to leave on your children's hearts and what do you need to do to be sure that's exactly the imprint you're leaving?
14. Are you living your life in such a way that your children will rise up and call you blessed?

11

ALWAYS A MOM

And these words that I command you today shall be on your heart.
You shall teach them diligently to your children, and shall talk of them
when you sit in your house, and when you walk by the way,
and when you lie down, and when you rise.
DEUTERONOMY 6:6-7, *ESV*

Parenting is rarely easy, but just when a mom thinks she has figured out how to mother her toddler, the sands of time shift and she has to learn how to parent a kindergartener. Navigating the ever-changing tide of time makes it hard for a mother to get a grip on parenting. Friends may come and go during the course of a child's life, but a mom is always a mom. "Always a Mom" takes mothers on a journey through the various stages of a child's life and clarifies her role along the way. This chapter is woven with real stories and biblical insight that will equip moms to pave the way for a lifelong relationship with the children in whom they have poured their lives.

Everything Changes

Motherhood is fluid, ever-evolving and constantly calling you to change the way you approach each season of it. From newborns to the empty nest, motherhood changes with each new age and stage of your child's life. The journey is messy and we worry about messing up our kids along the way.

Ruth Bell Graham once said, "In raising children, all you can do is your best . . . we take care of the possible and leave the impossible to God."

In the early days of mommy-hood, your life is filled with sleepless nights, dirty diapers and a mounting pile of spit-up-laden baby bibs. Then you shift to toddler-hood and you quickly forget what it means to sit still for five minutes, you're on guard for everything they put in their mouths, and you discover the real-life definition of a temper tantrum.

As the years pass, your child moves from preschool age to kindergarten and from elementary age to the tweens and teen years, and all the while, your life evolves with theirs.

Each age and each stage comes with different parenting challenges. And just when you think you've got it down, you have another child or the child you have moves into a new stage of life.

Ages and Stages

Babies learn so much more than we realize by the time they are two. Those who nurture them are the ones who help form their concept of whether or not they can trust others. Schedules provide an important sense of structure and security. Mommas may be consumed with cooking, cleaning, bathing, burping and feeding, but how sweet to know each selfless act contributes to their children's confidence in their parents, and their perception of the world around them.

From two to three years old, children are discovering self-control, a bit about responsibility, and a keen awareness of boundaries. This is when potty-training and temper tantrums can leave a momma wondering what in the world she's supposed to do. It's a time when consistency is key and kids discover their natural ability to push their parent's limits to try to get their way.

Some people call this the terrible twos. My oldest son was super-compliant, but this was when my youngest son's constant battle of the wills crept up and caught me off guard. Wow! It wasn't easy and he was as strong-willed as strong-willed gets. Unfortunately, I didn't have the whole intentional parenting thing down and I lost the war of wills more times than I'd like to admit. But when I was consistent with his boundaries and I didn't resort to yelling, I would win. After all . . . I was the mom. Right? Right!

And so are you. If you find yourself in this season of parenting, don't let it overwhelm you. Set those reasonable boundaries and stick to your guns. Teaching your children the concept of consequences will help them become responsible adults as well as help them develop the priceless ability to reason for themselves.

During the preschool years, from three to about five, kids begin developing a stronger sense of right from wrong while also cultivating their own creativity. These are great years to feed their imagination through innovative crafts, games, sports and other activities, while consistently setting boundaries and providing opportunities for them to reason things out.

Throughout the elementary school ages (from 6 to 11), kids are growing in a multitude of areas and have a whole host of new needs. They are developing social skills, navigating relationships, longing for a sense of belonging and approval, acquiring a sense of success and achievement; and yet, they still love playing with their toys, sitting in mommy's lap, and they still need momma to kiss their booboos and tuck them in at night.

The teen years are often very tumultuous—not only for the parents, but for the teens too. These are the years when kids struggle with their identity. Who are they? What tribe do they fit in? They seek acceptance from their peers and, unfortunately, what others think about them has the propensity to outweigh much of what you've taught them all their lives. During these difficult years, there is no substitute for creating an open line of communication. Kids don't always want to talk about what is going on in their lives, so parents have to prayerfully and carefully treasure those times when they do.

Below is an acronym that might help you as you enter into these awkward years when you may begin wondering where that sweet little child you raised is hiding. The acronym is S.H.A.P.E. Every time you have an open window of conversation, you have the chance to SHAPE your child's heart.

- S—Speak wisely: They really want to know what you think, but choose your words wisely.
- H—Hear them intently: Much of what they say is found between the lines.

- A—Analyze cautiously: Your kids don't need your judgment; they need your wisdom, compassion and unconditional love. This doesn't mean you don't correct bad behavior or continue to instill right from wrong; it just means that you do so without coming across as judgmental and condemnatory.
- P—Parent intentionally: Carefully consider your response and parent with the ultimate purpose of helping them become all God created them to be.
- E—Encourage consistently: Never stop being your child's biggest cheerleader as you consistently encourage them in their true identity.

These are the years when you have to be strong, sweet momma. Your children may want you to accept them when they haven't even discovered who they really are. Your job is to believe in who you know they are while inspiring them to become all God created them to be.

As you know, motherhood is messy and it constantly calls you to adapt, improvise, reflect and strategize—just when you think you've got parenting down, your children enter a new stage and you feel like you're starting over.

Everything changes, sweet mom! And as you grow with your kids, please remember that God has equipped you for this! Through Christ, you are exactly the mother your child needs for every age and every stage.

Lori's Story

When Lori's kids where toddlers, she loved to use two techniques: distraction and humor. Distracting her kids helped her minimize the common two-year-old power struggle. Lori knew that if her children were wearing her out with whining, trying their best to get their way, or getting out of hand with the get-me-that comments in the store, if she could distract them and get their attention on something else, or if she could make them laugh, then she would win the battle of the wills.

Those were her go-to parenting strategies when her kids were tiny tots. Then came that dreadful moment when the gig was up.

"Mom, I know you're just trying to detrack [distract] me."

She knew she was busted and it was time to develop a new approach to parenting her ever-maturing children. And as with most kids, no two are the same, so what worked for one did not work for the other. Each child calls us to parent differently and it's really hard to be an expert parent when there is no clear-cut rulebook.

Lori learned the importance of being flexible with each new age and stage of parenting. Sometimes that's hard. Sometimes we don't get it right. Okay . . . so, many times we don't get it right. We can't be perfect parents and we won't always do the right thing, but God is the perfect Parent and we can seek His will and His wisdom for our kids as we navigate the parenting waters from newborns to the empty nest.

Lessons from the Empty Nest

The empty nest. Some parents anxiously await it, other parents avoid even thinking about it, but it eventually comes for every parent on the planet.

I know one dad who was super excited about the fact that his son was headed off to college and he didn't waste any time making a man cave out of his son's bedroom. Another dad sat on his daughter's bed and cried for hours after his baby girl moved out of their home and into an apartment with a friend.

One mom was thrilled that she could start making plans to travel around the world when her last child left the nest. Another mom puttered around the house, depressed for days after her daughter married the man of her dreams and began her new life as a wife.

Moms may differ in the way they handle life when their children fly the coop, but there are great lessons to be learned from the empty nest by moms of all ages. It wasn't until my boys were grown and gone when I discovered that we never stop being a mom. I mean, I knew I would always be my sons' mom, but experience has a way of teaching us the depth of what words cannot.

I remember when I was in my early twenties and my mom would say, "Stephanie, you have no idea what you put me through when you do things like that!" To be honest, I had no clue why what

I did mattered to her and I really didn't give it a second thought. But when my boys became men, it didn't take long for me to figure out that my mom was right. A mom never stops being a mom.

Everything they go through, we go through it with them. Every bad decision they make, they drag their momma's heart through it right along with them. It doesn't matter if they live close or across the world, God has given us a mom heart that time and distance cannot change.

One day while I was sitting outside to soak up a little sunshine, I noticed a little rustling in the branches above my head. I looked up and saw a momma bird nudging her babies out of their nest. There, in my own back yard, was a National Geographic moment in the making. It was painful to watch as those baby birds desperately tried to cling to the wiry branches that had once been meticulously put in place by their parents. It was their home . . . it was all they had ever known . . . it was where they grew up in the twig-lined tree house suspended by two limbs. But now it was time for them to soar and discover that there was a whole wide world awaiting them just beyond their little bungalow in the tree.

Soaring. It was what they were created for. As I sat there gazing at the momma's struggle to send them off, I was reminded of a night not long after my nest was empty and my heart was hurting. Perched beside the window, I peered out between the blinds with tears in my eyes and my sons on my mind. My boys had become men, and life as I had known it had dramatically changed. I know that's how it's supposed to be, but the silence can be deafening.

I loved every minute of having my children at home. Even in the difficult times. They were safe in our little bungalow made with cinderblock walls and ceramic tile floors. It was a place where laughter echoed through each room and joy filled the air. It was where we did our best to fortify their faith and challenge them to stand strong in troubled times. It's where we taught them right from wrong, laughed together, cried together, and tucked them in at night with precious butterfly kisses.

For 11 years, I was a homeschool mom. Eleven years of book fairs, planning curriculum, organizing field trips, teaching at our local homeschool co-op—but best of all was treasured time with my sons.

And then one day it all came to a screeching halt and I was hurled like a discus into a new season of life. I'm not sure why, but I never realized that the empty nest was the goal. As I looked back in the rearview mirror of my motherhood journey, I couldn't help but wonder what I would have done differently. Here are just a few things that I would have done differently—things that would have made for more intentional parenting:

- I would have worked harder at parenting the adult they would become and not just the child they were.
- I would have searched more diligently for a mentor to help me in my journey as a mom.
- I would have looked for more ways to strengthen their talents and feed their dreams.
- I would have definitely bought that camcorder we thought we couldn't afford and captured those Kodak moments for generations to come.
- I think I would have taken Midol so that my children wouldn't have had to experience my monthly hormonal meltdowns.
- I would have taken more trips to the park and spent more days at the beach.
- I would have basked in the beauty of a midnight sky as we counted the stars and conversed about the Creator.
- I would have spent less time cleaning the grout between my tile, scrubbing the baseboards and organizing the linen closet.
- I would have never told them to quit laughing.

I'm not sure how the years flew by so fast or when my boys became men, but I know I miss them like crazy every day. It's ironic, but the empty nest is really the goal; and yet, when our children are home all snug in their beds and life revolves around baseball practice and guitar lessons, we don't even give it a second thought.

One day, sweet mom, it will be your children's turn to soar. It's what they were created for. Your job is to prepare them to trust God for their journey, to teach them how to fly above their circumstances, how to keep their wings strong, how to keep their hearts clean, and how to find shelter from the storm under the shadow of the Almighty when the winds begin to batter their soul and weaken their resolve.

They may soar, but you'll always be their mom and there's nothing like watching them take flight and begin fulfilling the plan God has for their lives.

Holly's Story

When Holly's son was 15, she couldn't help but wonder where the years had gone. It seemed like just yesterday when she stood outside her baby's bedroom door with tears streaming down her face while her son cried inside the room because he didn't want to take a nap. Her baby boy needed a nap, but it broke her heart to hear him cry. Eventually, he fell asleep and when he woke up there wasn't a trace of a tear, only a face that lit up the room like sunshine, ready to take on the day.

Holly's guilt was heavy and being a mom was hard. Making a baby take a nap because you know he needs one, making a child clean his room because he needs to learn responsibility, telling a teen she can't text message past 9:00 PM because you want to protect her influence and innocence, can all heap loads of guilt on a momma's heart.

It was during those times when her parenting choices seemingly broke her son's little heart that Holly made her way to her quiet place where she would begin digging deep in the Word seeking God's will and God's ways. It was during those times when Holly's heart was heavy and she felt like an incompetent parent that she would plant her heart in the Word of God and ask the Lord to shed some biblical light on what a good momma really looks like.

One day, Holly situated herself in her 15-year-old son's room and reflected on years gone by as she wrote these words:

Today, I sit in your room, praying over you and the struggles you face. It's funny how you hold on to the keepsakes from those early years—displaying them in your room. I have my own keepsakes too, but you can't put them in picture frames because they are written on my heart.

I pray over the new level of challenges you are about to face—the up and down emotions of a freshman boy finding his way as a man.

Every day we are giving you more tools to self-monitor and make choices. We are taking steps to secure you and guard your path as best we can. However, I find that the struggles are not much different today than they were when we were your age. We too had to learn how to say no. And so we teach you to do the same for your own good. We are called to set boundaries, even when you moan and groan over them.

"No, your friend cannot come over." "Yes, you need to limit your playing games to this amount of time." "I know you hate technology-free days, but Daddy is reading a great book you like!" "No, you cannot go to the retreat. I know it's for youth group, but it's a lot of money and we can't afford it."

The parental guilt I feel has lessened over the years because I understand the good that will come from a well-thought-out no. It is for the best. You are becoming a set-apart young man, walking in all God's ways. The constraints we place upon you, though hard at times, are training you for your own battles one day. You are finding that the freest place you can grow is under the authority of God, with rules and statutes that are for you.

Oh, you want to be a soldier? Well, march on, dear son, and stay in the Word! Your mama will continue to dig deeper in Scripture for every season and its challenges, knowing that only God can teach us both.

The years have taught Holly some monumental lessons in motherhood—the kind of stuff that only time can teach and desperate hearts can learn. It won't be long before her son is out of the nest, but until then, Holly and her hubby enjoy treasured time with their boy, knowing that the years will fly by and he will soon be marching on his own.

The Legacy of Motherhood

Many mothers who have gone before us have left a legacy of mommyhood worth following; others . . . not so much. But whether the pathway they paved was good or bad, there are lessons we can learn from them. Let's look at a few:

Eve

Beyond the Garden of Eden and not long after the fall of man, Eve became pregnant and motherhood was born. How fitting that Eve's name means life. She is not only the mother of all mothers, but also every human who has ever lived can trace their ancestry back to her.

Sometimes I can't help but wonder how she did it. She didn't know what motherhood looked like. After all, she didn't have a mom or a mentor. No example to follow, no one who could answer those desperate questions mommas ask when they feel they aren't getting it right.

There was no Bible she could turn to for words of wisdom, no local bookstore where parenting books lined the shelves, and no physiologists or parenting experts to help her figure it out.

Eve was a trailblazer—the pioneer of motherhood. And with untold numbers of children to raise, this trail was hers to blaze on her own. The only help she was going to get was from her equally clueless husband and the God whom she had sinned against but must desperately depend on now.

Scripture doesn't divvy out the details about those early years when Cain and Abel played with their hand-carved toys and Adam taught them how to grow crops and hunt for their next meal. We don't read about dinner around the table and the laughter that once filled their home. But what we do know about her beloved boys has taught us that motherhood is not for sissies.

Like all children, Eve's first two children were very different, and it didn't take long for her to learn that no matter what a momma does, her children don't always turn out the way she hopes they will.

> Cain spoke to Abel his brother. And when they were in the field, Cain rose up against his brother Abel and killed him (Gen. 4:8, *ESV*).

For some reason, I would have thought that the mother of all mothers would get a pass on pain. But Eve experienced a mother's ultimate tragedy when sibling rivalry gave way to rage and one son rose up against the other and killed him.

Throughout her lifetime, Eve gave birth to many more children, but nothing could ever change the fact that she lost one to death and the other to his own destructive choices. Once a mother, always a mother, whether those children are living or dead, whether those children are walking with God or paving their path with destructive choices.

Jochebed

During dangerous times, a faithful young Jewish woman gave birth to a beautiful baby boy. In an attempt to save his life, she placed him in a basket and sent him downstream directly into the arms of a childless princess. It was a risk she had to take and a demonstration of faith that beckons moms throughout the ages to trust God with their children.

She may have released her child, but through a God-ordained twist of fate, Jochebed became her own son's nursemaid. I'm sure mothering Moses didn't look like anything she had hoped it would, but Jochebed made the best of a bad situation and was able to experience the joy of raising her son.

Parenting doesn't always look the way we hoped it would. Physical, mental and emotional disabilities make our realities very different than the dreams we once tucked deep inside our momma hearts.

Challenging circumstances may wear a momma out and leave her feeling overwhelmed, but they don't change who she is or her love for her children. Instead, they often serve to reveal how relentless a mother's love can be.

Scripture is full of moms we can learn from. Some good. Some very bad.

1. Through Hannah, we learn to pray like crazy for our kids and surrender them to the Lord. (See 1 Sam. 1–2.)
2. Rebekah teaches us that playing favorites with our children is never a good idea and always comes with consequences. (See Gen. 27.)
3. Sarah gives us a glimpse of how important a momma's protective instincts can be. (See Gen. 21.)

4. Herodias gives us a look at the heart of a wicked momma who sowed wickedness in her own daughter's heart. (See Matt. 14.)
5. Timothy's mom and grandmother give us great examples of what it means to pour our faith into our children. (See 2 Tim. 1.)

It's not easy being a mom. We don't always know what to do, and as our children change, so must we. But no matter how young or old they are, you will always be their mom.

A Prayer for Mom

Precious Father, motherhood is a journey that will last the rest of my life. As long as I'm breathing, I will never stop being a mom, so please help me identify and intentionally parent my children well and give me a clear understanding in each age and stage they go through as they grow up. Enable me to transition as time transforms my children into adults. Lord, help me to not be caught off guard when my children move from one stage to another and please give me the wisdom to know what boundaries to set, what freedoms to give, and how to minister to their hearts with each age and stage of their lives. Precious Father, I'm always going to be their mom, so please help me in this lifelong journey called motherhood.

More for Mom

Everything Changes
1. At what age and stage are your children?
2. What help did you find in reading about the ages and stages of children?
3. If you have a teenager, how could the acronym S.H.A.P.E. help you with your children?

Lori's Story
4. Do you remember a time when your children caught on to one of your parenting techniques?

5. How do you need to change your parenting strategies to adjust to your child's stage of life?

Lessons from the Empty Nest

6. What lessons from the empty nest spoke to you most?
7. How can you begin preparing your children to soar right now?
8. How can you parent more intentionally today?

Holly's Story

9. Holly's son was 15 when she sat in his room and wrote him a letter. Take a few minutes and write a letter to your child(ren).

The Legacy of Motherhood

10. Why is it hard to parent children who are so different?
11. What did you learn from Eve?
12. What did you learn from Jochebed?
13. Take a minute and read about some of the other mothers listed and share what you learned from them.
14. How does knowing you are always a mom affect the way you think about yourself and your children?

PARENTING FROM YOUR KNEES

All your children shall be taught by the Lord,
and great shall be the peace of your children.
ISAIAH 54:13, *ESV*

Mom. She is a child's biggest cheerleader and most relentless prayer warrior. No one will ever want as much for her children as their mom does and no one will ever pray for them like she will. Using stories of real moms (some who have gone before us, others who are modern-day moms), "Parenting from Your Knees" will not only inspire mothers to see the significance of their consistent prayers for their children, but it will also provide them with specific prayers using the Word of God for every day of the month.

Mommas Who Prayed Powerful Prayers

From the dawn of history, mothers have loved their children as no one else could and prayed for them as no one else would.

Augustine is known as one of the early theologians of the faith. His mother, Monica, was the mother of three and the wife of a very malicious man. Like many, Augustine spent his younger years in pursuit of purpose. In his search for significance, he tried everything from wine to women to philosophy. But nothing seemed to satisfy.

When Augustine was about 35 years old, he became a Christian. He is noted as saying that he remembered his momma's prayers and in his autobiography, *Confessions*, he shared that his mother "wept to [God] for me, shedding more tears for my spiritual death than other mothers shed for the bodily death of a son." Augustine's powerful influence is still felt today.

Susanna Wesley raised 10 children. She was known to pray for two hours a day and frequently slipped into a private place to pray even more. Her sons John and Charles started the Methodist church and became world changers for the Lord Jesus Christ.

Hudson Taylor's mom consistently sought God's face for her son. One day she shut the door behind her and resolved not to leave until her prayers were answered. That day Hudson Taylor gave his life to Christ and lived to turn China upside down for Christ.

Hannah was barren, yet she prayed for a son. God answered that prayer and she gave her baby boy back to God. His name was Samuel and he went on to become a godly and influential prophet, priest and judge.

George Washington's dad died when George was only 10 years old, but his mother left a legacy of faith that would echo through the portals of history. She was known to pray diligently for her children; and before George left home, she gave him these important words of wisdom: "Remember that God is our only sure trust. To Him I commend you." And she added, "My son, neglect not the duty of secret prayer."

George went on to survive countless battles throughout the Revolutionary war and become the first president of the United States. As he reflected on the place from where God had brought him and what God had brought him to, he said, "My mother was the most beautiful woman I ever saw. All I am I owe to my mother. I attribute all my success in life to the moral, intellectual and physical education I received from her."

Ruth Bell Graham was the mother to three daughters and two sons. With her husband, Billy, who was often on the road, Ruth had her hands and her heart full. She was a fervent prayer warrior who relentlessly lifted her kids up to the Lord. It wasn't easy and they all didn't enter adulthood with the same passionate pursuit for God as their parents.

For several years, Franklin lived the life of a prodigal son until he gave his life to Christ in his early twenties. Today, he leads the Billy Graham Evangelistic Association as well as Samaritan's Purse.

Throughout history, moms have prayed for their children like no one else could or would and, in answer to their prayers, men and women of God have accomplished the impossible. Many of their children have attributed success to the faithful, fervent prayers of their mother.

You've heard it said that behind every great man there is a great woman. I believe that behind every great man or woman is a praying parent, grandparent or great-grandparent.

As I sit here thinking about each of you who will be reading this, I can't help but wonder what your mom, grandma or some distant relative has prayed for you. How many prayers have been lifted up for your salvation, for your future, for your provisions, for your protection?

When I was 27 years old, I went in search of my birth mom. It wasn't long before I found her, and after we met she told me she had been praying for me my whole life. She prayed for my salvation, protection, and that one day we would meet again.

She was a powerful prayer warrior who prayed like crazy for her kids and for everyone she met. Wherever she went, she asked complete strangers how she could pray for them. She wrote their names down, transferred them to her main prayer list, and when she got home began to pray for them as if she had known them all her life. When I typed out her handwritten list, there were over 700 names!

Found jotted down on the bottom of her mega-prayer list was this prayer: "I bind anyone not sent of God from entering my life, my children's lives, grandchildren's lives or my friend's lives. We won't have any counterfeits, fakes or false intruders. They will not touch our anointing or our ministries in any way, shape or form."

Her name was Faye Salvatierra. She wasn't famous and she never won any big awards. She never wrote a book and she never stood before thousands. But she left a legacy of faith that will forever be etched on the hearts of those she knew and loved.

She's with Jesus now and her faith has been made sight, but her prayers will touch the heart of God throughout eternity. She was a gentle woman who believed God for the impossible and prayed like she knew He was listening . . . because He was.

He is listening to you too, sweet mom. So, pray on!

Their Biggest Cheerleader

Okay, I admit it! I'm crazy about my kids and I love being a mom! I haven't always done it right and it definitely hasn't been easy, but throughout every age and stage of my children's lives, I have *loved* being a mom!

I remember standing on the sidelines when my oldest played ball, cheering him on as he lunged laterally through the air to catch a line drive. My heart pounded with pride as he snagged the ball in mid air, tucked it into his chest and fell to the ground. I was definitely the loudest mom there, but I couldn't help myself. I could feel what his little heart was feeling and I was as excited as he was.

When he struck out or missed the ball, I was still his biggest cheerleader and I was still the loudest mom in the bleachers. "It's all right, son. You'll get the next one! Everyone misses sometimes!"

When my youngest son stood behind the mic with a guitar in his hands and a song of praise on his lips as he led his peers in worship, my heart gushed. Not just because I was a proud mom (although that was definitely part of it), but also because I could feel what he was feeling and I was cheering him on in my heart.

Mommas are their children's biggest cheerleaders. We don't just cheer our children on when they do good or when their hearts have been hurt; we also cheer them on even when they behave badly. We don't give them a pass on bad behavior, but when we have to dole out the discipline, we still try to cheer them on to be all God created them to be.

Think about when you had your baby. As soon as your little bundle of joy was born, you knew deep down in your heart that no one could ever love that little one as much as you. Immediately, you became your baby's biggest cheerleader. Perhaps when children are born, hospitals should hand out pompoms with a card that reads, "Go ahead! We know you're going to need these."

When they do good, you're the one who cheers the loudest. When they blow it, you're the one who whispers words of encouragement to their hearts. When they misbehave, you're the one cheering them on to do better and choose right the next time.

My boys may now be men, but I've never stopped being their biggest cheerleader. Always have been. Always will be. Unfortunately, it takes a lot more than being their biggest cheerleader for them to become all God created them to be. We can't change their hearts, but we can pray to the One who can. We can't control their lives, but we can cry out to the One who is in complete control.

We may not like to think about it—maybe we don't even realize it—but we are in a war and the battle for our children won't be won with guns and knives. It will be won on our knees.

> For we do not wrestle against flesh and blood, but against the rulers, against the authorities, against the cosmic powers over this present darkness, against the spiritual forces of evil in the heavenly places (Eph. 6:12, *ESV*).

Our knees. It's where we fight for our kids most. It's the place where we stand in the gap for them and where we pray for them when they can't or won't pray for themselves. Every need they have, every character trait we long to see in their lives, every trial they go through, and every doubt and fear they face will best be met by the perfect Parent, our heavenly Father.

With all my heart, I long to see my sons step into their God-given destinies. And while I may be their biggest cheerleader, I'm not a perfect parent. I won't always get it right. I won't always say and do the right things. In the middle of a mommy meltdown moment, I'm prone to lose my patience and my mind.

I'm flawed and fallible, but God is not. And so I seek the face of the perfect Parent who never blows it. He never misunderstands a situation. He never blames the wrong child. He never overreacts or is overwhelmed. He never has meltdown moments and He is never at a loss as to what to do.

He alone can change hearts, lives and circumstances. He alone can weave together everything my children go through for their good. He alone can make beauty out of ashes, and no matter how much I think I love my kids, He loves them more.

It's a Scary World, Lord!

It was just a commercial—a silly 30-second slot on primetime TV that caused my heart to sink and my jaw to drop. As I stood there motionless, staring at my 32-inch screen, I realized I was going to be at war for the rest of my life. Little eyes shouldn't be exposed to sex scenes, random violence, and vulgar words that even an adult shouldn't see or hear. But in a blink of an eye, my little fella got a glimpse of an image that had the potential to be etched in his mind for the rest of his life.

After tucking my boys into bed, I sat on the couch, stared at the wall and thought, *It's a scary world, Lord! What am I going to do? How can I protect them from all of this? Wow, Lord! Parenting sure seemed a lot easier before I had kids!*

In a world where sex sells, where there are no moral absolutes, and where the fear of God is next to nonexistent, I knew that parenting my children to live godly lives was going to be much more difficult than I ever imagined. So, what's a mom to do when she can't control everything her children see, hear and are tempted by? What's a mom to do when she realizes she is raising her children in a very scary world?

We pray! We pray to the only One who can make all the difference in the world. We pray to the One who says "fear not" over 300 times in His Word. We pray to the One who loves our kids more than we do. We pray to the One who has a perfect plan for their lives. We pray to the One who promises never to leave or forsake us. We pray to the One who says that our mustard-seed-sized faith can move mountains. We pray to the One who intentionally placed our children in our specific family on purpose and for a purpose.

You may be a scared momma living in a scary world, but God knows your greatest fears, your deepest desires, your biggest doubts, and your grandest failures. He knows who your kids are, what they need, what they fear, what He is calling them to, what He will see them through, and how to get hold of their hearts.

I know it's a scary world, but we don't have to always have all the right answers; we only need to know how to get ahold of the One who is . . . and who does.

So, How Do I Pray for My Kids?

Prayer can seem daunting. Almost elusive. I remember not long after I became a Christian, I desperately wanted to hear how people prayed so that I could learn how to pray correctly. I thought there was some magic formula to a powerful prayer life and I desperately desired to be like one of those prayer warriors I had read about, especially for my children. So, I attended prayer meetings and carefully listened to the prayers of those who were older and wiser in the faith. I loved listening to the prayers that were uttered with eloquence by the older and wiser Christians. But the ones that flowed from the lips of new believers were just as powerful and just as beautiful. Their words weren't fancy, but their hearts were pure.

There, I discovered that God doesn't call us to fancy words or perfect prayers. He calls us to intimacy. He invites us to enter into His presence, sit at His table and dine with Him daily. It's an open invitation. He leaves the choice to say yes entirely up to us. It's the place where we meet with Him, where we bask in the beauty of His presence, where we lift up the longings of our heart, and where we stand in the gap for our kids and for those we know and love.

Prayer. It's the key to heaven's door and you are invited in any time. But prayer isn't always easy. In fact, Oswald Chambers said, "Prayer is the greater work." Sometimes, I've found myself treating prayer as if it's a spare tire. I take it out when I need it and put it away when all is well.

It's not always easy to find time to pray, especially for busy moms who daily finds themselves knee-deep in diapers, dishes and doctors' appointments. So, you may be wondering, *When? When can I find time to pray?*

You find it in the intentional moments before your kids wake up in the morning or you steal 30 minutes while your children play outside or you grab 20 minutes when you put them down for a nap, while they are at a friend's house or right after you tuck them into bed at night.

It's not easy, but it is definitely doable. As with mine, your prayer life may look more like a stumble than a walk, but it's one journey you don't want to miss for the world.

Practical Help for Powerful Prayers

Well, sweet mom, let's get practical about prayer. I don't have all the answers and I'm still discovering more ways to pray for my children, but I do want to share with you three things that I have learned along the way that have helped me become a better prayer warrior for my kids.

1. Cover Your Kids in Prayer

- *Pray for their spiritual needs*—Pray passionately for their salvation. It's their number one need. Pray for protection, direction and a heart after God. Pray that they will always have eyes to see, ears to hear and a heart to believe. Pray that they will be strong, courageous and relentless servants for Christ.
- *Pray for their emotional needs*—Pray for their emotional well-being. Pray that they will be strong without becoming hard, tender but not weak. Pray that they will understand their value and identity in Christ, that they will not be quickly angered or hold grudges. Pray that they will live and love well.
- *Pray for their physical needs*—Pray for their health. Pray that they will have disciplined eating and exercise habits. Pray that they will not have addictive behaviors.
- *Pray for their friends, coworkers and acquaintances*—Pray that God will surround them with people who will strengthen their faith, encourage their walk with God and hold them accountable. Pray that God will use them to make a difference in the lives of those they know. Pray that God will prepare your child's future spouse to be one who loves the Lord and who will love your child with the love of Christ.
- *Pray for their parents*—Yes, pray for yourself. Pray that you will be the example to your children that God calls you to be—that you will understand them, see their weaknesses, sins and needs, and will know how to walk them through each season of their childhood. Ask the Lord to give you the wisdom you need to parent them well.

2. Pray God's Word

Claim His promises, pray Scripture over your kids, and pray Scripture with your kids. When your children are struggling with being bossy, pray Luke 22:26 (*ESV*) for them: "Lord, you said that, 'Those who are greatest among you should take the lowest rank, and the leader should be like a servant.' Please help my children have a humble heart of service and make them the servant leaders You created them to be."

When you are praying for your children to have self-control, pray Galatians 5:23 and Proverbs 25:28: "Lord, in Galatians 5:23, You tell us that one of the fruits of the Spirit is self-control, and You say in Proverbs 25:28 that those who lack self-control are like a city whose walls are broken down. Please help my children walk in the Spirit and display the fruit of self-control so that they won't be like that city with broken-down walls—weak, vulnerable and unprotected."

Pray that your children will be taught of the Lord and that He will give them wisdom and direction according to Isaiah 54:13: "All your children shall be taught by the Lord, and great shall be the peace of your children."

The Bible is full of precious promises, precepts and principles that we can pray for and with our children. Below is a chart with a few examples that will help you discover the power of praying God's Word with and for your kids.

Prayer	Verse
Salvation	John 3:16 (*ESV*)—"For God so loved the world, that he gave his only Son, that whoever believes in him should not perish but have eternal life." 2 Peter 3:9 (*ESV*)—"The Lord is not slow to fulfill his promise as some count slowness, but is patient toward you, not wishing that any should perish, but that all should reach repentance." *Lord, help my children recognize their sins and ask You for forgiveness. I pray that, according to Your will, they will place their faith in Jesus as the Lord of their lives and the giver of eternal life.*

Prayer	Verse
Strong Faith	1 Corinthians 16:13 (*ESV*)—"Be watchful, stand firm in the faith, act like men, be strong." Ephesians 3:16 (*ESV*)—"that according to the riches of his glory he may grant you to be strengthened with power through his Spirit in your inner being." *Lord, help my children be watchful, stand firm in the faith and be strong. According to the riches of your glory, please strengthen my children with Your power through Your Spirit in their inner being.*

Prayer	Verse
Friendships	Proverbs 13:20 (*ESV*)—"Whoever walks with the wise becomes wise, but the companion of fools will suffer harm." 1 Samuel 18:1 (*ESV*)—"the soul of Jonathan was knit to the soul of David, and Jonathan loved him as his own soul." *Lord, please help my children choose wise friends and avoid those who are foolish. Surround them with those who love You, and give them those rare and special friendships that will last a lifetime. Friends who will tell them what they need to hear, not just what they want to hear.*

Prayer	Verse
Future Spouse	1 Corinthians 6:14 (*ESV*)—"Do not be unequally yoked with unbelievers. For what partnership has righteousness with lawlessness? Or what fellowship has light with darkness?" Genesis 2:24 (*ESV*)—"Therefore a man shall leave his father and his mother and hold fast to his wife, and they shall become one flesh." *Lord, please prepare the heart of my child's future wife. Give her a heart after you. Keep my child from wanting anyone except the one You have for him. Help him not desire someone who doesn't know You and help him be prepared to be the husband he needs to be for his future wife.*

Prayer	Verse
Friendships	Ephesians 6:11 (*ESV*)—"Put on the whole armor of God, that you may be able to stand against the schemes of the devil." James 4:7 (*ESV*)—"Submit yourselves therefore to God. Resist the devil, and he will flee from you." *Lord, please remind my children to consistently put on the armor of God so that they can stand against the schemes of the enemy. Give them a heart that is submissive to You and that resists the enemy so that the enemy will have to flee.*

3. Pray for their Character by Using Biblical Characters

- *David*—Pray that your children will have a heart like David, a heart that longs for the living God (see Acts 13:22). Pray that they will become men and women of faith and courage (see 1 Sam. 17:45), men and women who wait patiently on God and delight to do His will (see Ps. 40), and that they will become men and women of faithful repentance (see Ps. 51).
- *Moses*—Pray that your children will have a heart of humility like Moses (see Num. 12:3), that they will become friends of God (see Jas. 2:23). Pray that they will choose what is right over what is easy (see Heb. 11:24-26).
- *Paul*—Pray that your children will be relentless in their faith and their callings regardless of how hard it gets, as Paul was (see 2 Cor. 11:23-28). Pray that they will count everything as worthless compared to knowing Christ (see Phil. 3:7-10), that they will stand for what is right (see Gal. 2:11), and that they will admit when they are wrong (see 2 Tim. 4:11).
- *Mary*—Pray that your children will be submissive to God's will even when it doesn't make sense, as was Mary (see Luke 1:48). Pray that they will be worshipers of God who are dependent upon Him (see Luke 1:46-55).

These are just a few examples of some ways my prayer life for my kids has evolved over the years. I make lists, use prayer calendars and write my prayers in my journal. These are all helpful tools in a momma's prayer arsenal to help us to pray for our kids. You may not use a calendar or you may not choose to journal your prayers, but whatever you do, pray on, sweet mom, pray on!

The Lord listens to the cry of a momma's heart and He loves your children more than you do! You may not see the Lord working in their lives today, but keep praying. Maybe their character still isn't what it should be. Keep praying. Maybe they have a big decision to make. Keep praying. Perhaps they're facing overwhelming peer pressure. Keep praying. When you see areas of weakness, need, doubt or fear, keep praying—keep standing in the gap for your kids.

There's power in your prayers, sweet momma! Stand in the gap for your kids and pray like no one else will. You are their biggest cheerleader and their most fervent prayer warrior, and if you don't pray, who will?

A Prayer for Mom

Precious Father, I know the most powerful place a mom can be is on her knees, and that the best thing I can do for my kids is to pray for them. Help me always be their biggest cheerleader and most relentless prayer warrior! Lord, You know I'm crazy about my kids, but I know that as much as I love them, You love them more! Help me consistently fight for my kids on my knees and stand in the gap for them when they can't or won't pray for themselves. Oh Lord, I know that we live in a scary world, that the enemy is real, and that their flesh is weak, but I also know You are God and there is nothing You can't do. Help me stand on Your Word and seek Your face for my kids, no matter how old they are and no matter what they are going through. As Oswald Chambers once said, "Prayer is the greater work." Help me pray on, no matter what!

More for Mom

Mommas Who Prayed Powerful Prayers

1. As you read through the moms who have prayed powerful prayers, are you inspired to become a strong prayer warrior for your children? If so, in what ways?
2. How did my birth mom's prayer life encourage you to pray more for your kids?

Their Biggest Cheerleader

3. What are some ways you can cheer on your kids when they are hurting, sad or afraid?
4. How can you cheer them on when they mess up?
5. Do you see yourself as your children's biggest cheerleader and how can you begin cheering for them from your knees?

It's a Scary World, Lord!

6. What are some things that scare you about the way the world is and the influence it can have on your children?
7. How does knowing that God knows and loves your children more than you do help you as a parent and in your prayer life?

So, How Do I Pray for My Kids?

8. What are some ways you can make time to pray for your children?

Practical Help for Powerful Prayers

9. How can the examples of praying for specific areas of your children's lives help you in your own prayers for your kids?
10. I shared just a few examples of how to pray for your kids using Scripture and Bible characters. How can you use these and other Scriptures to pray for your children?

ABOUT THE M.O.M. INITIATIVE

The M.O.M. Initiative is a comprehensive ministry devoted to helping the body of Christ make mentoring moms missional. Using M.O.M. as an acronym to describe the heart of this ministry, we are Mothers on a Mission to Mentor Other Mothers.

The M.O.M. Initiative provides biblical resources and support that give mentors and small-group leaders the confidence, courage and community they need to connect with other moms. It comes alongside local churches and ministries to help them minister to moms and the children they are raising through:

- M.O.M. Groups in local churches and ministries
- Helping churches and ministries make mentoring missional and practical by beginning M.O.M. Groups in neighborhoods, low-income apartment complexes, juvenile shelters, prisons, crisis pregnancy centers, and wherever young moms can be found
- Online support for moms and M.O.M. Group leaders
- Uniquely written biblical resources, planning guides, and training

The M.O.M. Initiative—reaching the moms of this generation so we can reach the heart of the next generation and change the world one mom at a time.

Website: www.themominitiative.com
Email: stephanie@themominitiative.com
Facebook: www.facebook.com/TheMOMInitiative
Twitter: @themominitiative

Appendix 2

THE MAKING OF A MOM **AND** THE M.O.M. INITIATIVE

Small-Group and M.O.M. Group Overview

Have you ever wished there was a book that could help moms navigate the difficult waters of motherhood from a biblical perspective, yet also serve as a tool that is specifically designed to make small-group study and mentoring moms easy and relevant?

The Making of a Mom does both. The M.O.M. Initiative incorporates *The Making of a Mom* as its premier resource to help the Body of Christ make mentoring missional.

The Making of a Mom was uniquely written to encourage a mom's heart in her journey and to serve as a church resource that will also answer the questions most would-be mentors and small-group leaders ask: *What will I do? What will I say? What will I use?*

The venue-specific "Planning Guides" in the back of *The Making of a Mom* help mentors and small-group leaders answer the question, "What will I do?"

The carefully crafted questions at the end of each chapter will help a mom reflect on her own journey and will also serve as a catalyst for conversation. *The Making of a Mom* answers the question, "What will I say?"

As a book written to meet mothers in the midst of their mom journey and provide a real-life look at biblical motherhood, *The Making of a Mom* helps moms answer the question, "What will I use?"

What Is The M.O.M. Initiative?

The M.O.M. Initiative is a fresh new vision for an age-old calling and we are dedicated to helping the Body of Christ make mentoring missional. We provide uniquely designed, mom-specific and mentor-friendly biblical resources, as well as support that gives mentors and small-group leaders the confidence, courage and community they need to connect with other moms.

The M.O.M. Initiative helps churches and ministries connect with each other and also connect with moms in their area to impact their communities and this culture for the Lord Jesus Christ.

Why The M.O.M. Initiative?

The M.O.M. Initiative exists because we all need each other and because being a mom isn't easy and children don't come with instructions.

The M.O.M. Initiative is a natural fit for any church or ministry, but it is also evangelistic in nature. We help churches reach young moms with the gospel of Jesus Christ, knowing that if we reach the moms of this generation, we will reach the heart of the next generation. But if we don't, we may just lose them all. So, we are asking the Church to join us as we reach moms for Christ and minister to those who already know Him.

What Does The M.O.M. Initiative Do?

The M.O.M Initiative helps you make mentoring a practical and missional reality in your church or ministry by:

- Providing Ministry Connection Worksheets online
- Providing practical and relevant resources for 6- to 12-week mom/mentor journeys
- Providing online support and an online database
- Providing training, organizational and M.O.M. Group materials
- Providing companion videos for resources, an optional schedule and icebreakers
- Providing ideas for how you can enhance your M.O.M. Group
- Providing venue-specific leader's guides and missional mentoring helps

What Is a M.O.M. Group and How Do I Begin One?

A M.O.M. Group is a gathering of moms of all ages who meet to do the mom journey together. It's Titus 2 in real life with a missional twist to help local churches and ministries reach their communities and this culture through the power and beauty of mentoring.

You can begin a M.O.M. Group as a small group in your church, or as a one-on-one organic relationship. Meet in a classroom, at the dining room table, at the park, at the local coffee shop, or whatever venue works best for you.

Using *The Making of a Mom* to begin your group will provide a 12-week mentoring experience during which you can not only establish and nurture your relationships with the young moms you are mentoring but also help them grow as mothers and in their walk with the Lord.

The ultimate heart of The M.O.M. Initiative is to help you make mentoring missional by inviting moms in your community to join and by partnering with local ministries such as those:

- in your community
- in low-income apartment complexes and neighborhoods
- in juvenile shelters and prisons
- through para-ministries such as crisis pregnancy centers, homes for unwed mothers, homeless shelters, women's shelters, MOPS, It's 4 uMom, and countless other ministries
- as a faith-based alternative for social service programs and court-appointed parenting classes
- on the mission field as a tool for missionaries to minister to moms
- in neighborhoods where individual moms begin organic mentoring relationships

Enhance your M.O.M. Group experience when possible by including practical skills such as:

- Recipes/Meal Making
- Resume Writing/Job Skills
- Sewing/Crafts
- Computer Skills

- Organizational Skills
- Budget/Financial Skills
- Educational/Tutoring
- CPR/Healthy Living

What Does a Typical M.O.M. Group Schedule Look Like?

Your M.O.M. Group will look different in different venues, especially with your missional M.O.M. Groups, but a typical M.O.M. Group schedule in a church/ministry or home might look something like this:

9:00 AM: Opening Prayer/Meet & Greet Icebreakers/
          K.I.D.s Group
9:15 AM: Practical Tip Time—Make a Meal/Learn Excel/
          Create a Budget
9:45 AM: M.O.M. to Mom Time (Study/Grow/Chat/
          Biblical Mommy-hood)
10:30 AM: Snack Food Fest/Chit-chat/Clean-up
10:45 AM: Pick up Children from K.I.D.s Group

How Do I Register My M.O.M. Group?

Register your church, ministry or yourself online as a M.O.M. Group and we will add you to our database. There is no fee to establish a M.O.M. Group, but we do accept donations.

Included in this book are Planning Guides for various venues to help you as you minister to moms in your church and your community. You will also need to register at www.themominitiative. com where your M.O.M. Group will be listed on our online database, making it easy for those looking for a mentor or a M.O.M. Group in your area to find you.

More About How to Begin a M.O.M. Group

A M.O.M. Group can have a simple start. Beginning a M.O.M. Group can be as simple as getting a handful of mentoring mommas together with some young mothers to start meeting on a weekly basis. You could gather as a weekly small group at church, as a Sunday school class, at your home, community center or local coffee shop. Find a spot that works best for you and the mom(s) you will be meeting with. Or you can begin your M.O.M. Group with a bang. If you are a church, para-church ministry or organization that would like a more structured, larger-scaled approach to beginning a M.O.M. Group, you will find a more comprehensive organizational structure and timeline below.

This is designed to help you have a great mentoring ministry that flows from your church into your community and changes the world one mom at a time.

Get started with an exciting kick-off and just remember, if you have any questions, the staff at The M.O.M. Initiative is here to help!

Three Months Prior to M.O.M. Group Kick-off Night

Establish who will serve as your M.O.M. Group leader(s). She will cast the vision for the women's ministry and be in contact with The M.O.M. Initiative for support, encouragement and information.

Meet and plan. The M.O.M. Group leader and women's ministry leaders gather together and discuss the opportunities to mentor moms in your church or ministry as well as through various ministry relationships in which the church is already involved. (In the back of this book, you will find Planning Guides for a variety of venues for possible missional mentoring opportunities in your area.)

Checklist

_____ Establish plans to launch a M.O.M. Group in your church.

_____ Consider how to invite Titus 2 women to join the revolution and begin mentoring moms within the church.

_____ Develop a plan to promote your new M.O.M. Group mentoring ministry. There are videos and promotional material available online at www.

themominitiative.com to help you get the word out and increase participation.

_____ Make a list of the ministries beyond your four walls that you can connect with to establish M.O.M. Groups.

_____ Make a list of possible mentoring venues and decide who will contact them to begin making arrangements for your new M.O.M. Group.

_____ Define plans that will work for your church and in your community.

_____ Remember, a M.O.M. Group is a great resource to use in your Single Moms ministry. *The Making of a Mom* is the perfect book to get your M.O.M. Group started.

_____ Establish a kick-off date approximately three months or so out.

_____ Begin organizing the M.O.M. Group kick-off banquet and developing a lead team for the M.O.M. Group kick-off. If possible, make it a church-wide activity for the women of the church.

_____ Invite a speaker who will speak on mentoring, or have your M.O.M. Group team leader be prepared to cast the vision for your M.O.M. Group and for reaching your community for Christ through mentoring. The M.O.M. Initiative has a list of exceptional, qualified speakers who are passionate about mentoring. You can visit the website (www.themominitiative.com) and find a speaker near you.

Two Months Prior to the M.O.M. Group Kick-off

_____ Let the promotions begin! It's time to get your promo material out so that you can get the word out about your M.O.M. Group!

_____ Start asking potential mentors and mentees to sign up. Continue promotion for about a month using videos, skits, website, Facebook and Twitter promotional resources.

_____ M.O.M. Group team get-togethers. It's time to talk about the contacts that have been made with potential mentoring venues, and confirm dates, times and things that still need to be completed.

_____ Continue working on the M.O.M. Group kick-off.

Six Weeks Prior to the M.O.M. Group Kick-off

_____ Meet with mentors for training. Start with The M.O.M. Initiative training video, then have The M.O.M. Initiative team leader share a Titus 2 Bible study and include personal mentoring stories if possible.

_____ Continue organizing the M.O.M. Group kick-off.

_____ Begin promoting your M.O.M. Group and invite potential mentors and mentees to sign up. Continue promotion using videos, skits, website, Facebook and Twitter promotional resources.

_____ Finalize your M.O.M. Group plans as well as your missional M.O.M. Group plans with the various venues where you will be establishing a M.O.M. Group.

Four Weeks Prior to the M.O.M. Group Kick-off

_____ M.O.M. team prayer gathering. Meet together with the mentors to pray over each other, for the ministry, for the moms in the church, for the various M.O.M. Groups, and for the venues your church will be involved in.

_____ Give the M.O.M. mentors their books. Find out if they understand how a M.O.M. Group works and if they have any questions.

_____ Touch base with the speaker to be sure everything is still a go and discuss any details you need to go over.

_____ Continue to finalize the kick-off plans.

_____ Work on seating plans to place mentors and mentees together.

_____ Create M.O.M. to mom icebreakers for the M.O.M. Group kick-off so that, as they sit at a table together, they will be able to get to know one another better during the M.O.M. Group kick-off.

_____ Be sure to have extra mentors at the kick-off for those mentees who sign up at the last minute.

M.O.M. Group Kick-off Day

_____ It's the big day, so don't let yourself get stressed out. Just let the fun begin!

_____ Enjoy the fun, the food, the M.O.M. to mom icebreakers and the speaker!

Three Months After the M.O.M. Group Kick-off

_____ Begin planning your M.O.M. Group celebration night. It can be held about four months after the kick-off. The M.O.M. Group celebration night is a great opportunity for the mentors and mentees to share their stories! It's a great night of encouragement, testimonies, fun, food, fellowship and a time to keep the M.O.M. Group momentum going!

_____ Plan to have new mentors and mentees sign up as well as those who have just finished their 12-week journey together. (Make your M.O.M. Group celebration night as easy as you possibly can by having finger foods or desserts.)

Four Months After the M.O.M. Group Kick-off (and a week to a month before your new M.O.M. Group session begins)

_____ Enjoy your M.O.M. Group celebration night. It's a time to have a blast celebrating what the

Lord has done and a time when mentors and mentees sign up for a new round of mentoring. The goal is to continue various mentoring ministries throughout the year, both there at the church and missionally. Some moms will not be able to do it all year, but others are looking forward to joining in the mentoring fun!

Quarterly or semiannual M.O.M. celebration nights will weave mentoring into the fabric of your women's ministry and help to keep mentoring at the forefront of the heart of the church. They will also constantly give new mentors an opportunity to join the revolution and make a difference as well as give young moms a chance to find a mentor who will be willing to walk them through what a mother is and what a mother does from a biblical perspective.

AN IMPORTANT LETTER TO M.O.M. GROUP LEADERS

You're my hero, sweet sister! You have chosen to step outside of your own world to enter the world of another. Not just for the sake of doing so, but also to make a difference. How beautiful to see God's girls fulfilling God's Titus 2 plan!

It takes time and effort to take on the role of a mentor, but the rewards are so worth it! Every moment you spend with your mentee, you have the awesome opportunity to impact two generations at the same time for the glory of God.

Below are a few tips to help you foster your newfound relationships in your M.O.M. Group:

1. Be prepared. Your diligence to prepare ahead of time is key to a successful mentoring relationship. If you are not able to do so, please do not take on this role. It will only frustrate you and hinder what you hope to accomplish.
2. Bring refreshments where permitted. Nothing breaks the ice like warm cookies and coffee. You don't have to bring a meal, but snacks have a way of creating a casual environment.
3. Be on time. Timeliness demonstrates respect for others. When you show up on time, you are simultaneously teaching respect and showing it.
4. Control the conversation. It's important to stay focused. You don't have to cover every question in the

Mentor Guide, but you will want to keep the conversation headed in the right direction.

5. Be accessible. Give your young mother your phone number and your permission to call you when she needs or wants to talk to you.

6. Be thoughtful. Call your young mother during the week and let her know you are thinking about her and praying for her. Send her a postcard, birthday card or anniversary card. Bring a small gift when you meet together. Little things show you care.

7. Be loving. Sincerely love your young mother. She will sense your Christ-like love and it will help validate what she learns during your time together.

8. Be prayerful. Pray for her throughout the week. Be sure to take prayer requests every time your group meets. Look for opportunities during the conversation to identify needs and let her know you are praying for her.

9. Be willing. If she doesn't have a car, you can offer to take her to the grocery store or to a doctor's appointment. Little gestures like that may be a bit inconvenient, but they demonstrate love as no words can.

10. Be friends. Remember, your goal as a mentor is not just to finish the book; it is to develop a long-term relationship with a young mother you hope will sense a special freedom to call you when she needs advice or prayer. Please don't allow the end of this book to be the end of your relationship. The M.O.M. Initiative is just a tool to use in the development of a long-lasting relationship. I hope you will continue growing closer and will flourish in your future fellowship.

Each time you meet together, be sure to start with a sincere, personal discussion about how the week went for both of you. Pray with her and for her. Remember, this is your opportunity to get to know each other better and do some bonding. (Don't forget to keep the focus primarily on her.)

I'm so thankful you have chosen to take this journey, my friend. I know you will never regret one moment of giving yourself away so that others may know Him more and become the best possible mothers they can be.

This is your opportunity to change the world one life at a time. It won't be easy, but it will be worth it. Oh yes—it will be worth it!

Be sure to go to www.themominitiative.com and click on the mentor tab. There you will find encouragement and creative ideas about your role as a mentor. You can also share your stories there about how God is working in your life as a mentor and in the life of your young mother.

Direct your young mother to www.themominitiative.com where she can find a daily dose of encouragement, resources and information covering topics from A to Z. She can also click on the mentee tab and find information that can help her in her journey as a mentee.

Through the website, your mentee will be part of a community of moms and can take part in discussions covering everything from practical parenting to fitness, recipes to spiritual growth, and from single moms to blended families. She will also be able to schedule an appointment for a private chat with a "virtual" mentor who can help her in her time of need.

The M.O.M. Initiative website is designed to offer a community experience and assist you in your role as a mentor and encourage the mentee beyond this book. Please be sure to register as a M.O.M. Initiative partner.

Please know that you have been the object of my prayers and have a special place in my heart. You really are my hero, and I can't wait to hear what God does in your life and in the life of the mom(s) you mentor through this journey. ❂

Appendix 4

BEYOND THE FOUR WALLS

The M.O.M. Initiative and M.O.M. Group Planning Guides

A Personal Message to Mentors

Hey, you! Yeah, you. Come closer. I want to tell you a secret. I really want to share my heart with you and explain what The M.O.M. Initiative ministry is all about. You see, it's not just a program; it's a revolution. That's right—it's a revolution of women who are courageous enough to take hold of their God-given Titus 2 identities—women who are willing to say yes with a passion to turn this world upside down.

We are mothers on a mission to mentor other mothers and we are linking hearts and hands to leave a legacy of faith, not only in our families and churches, but also in our communities and in this culture.

You've probably heard it said that the hand that rocks the cradle rules the world. If that's true, then I believe the church that mentors those hands will win the world. While each generation hangs in the balance between a mother's commitment to her calling and a world that distracts and detaches her from it, we are given the opportunity to make a multi-generational difference.

Although The M.O.M. Initiative will find a natural home within the church, it is not designed to remain confined within the church's four walls. The ultimate goal of The M.O.M. Initiative is to make mentoring intentionally missional so that the Body of Christ can impact the mothers within the church who will, in turn, desire to impact the mothers outside the church. It is a ripple effect of mothers who are on a mission to mentor other mothers. I hope you catch the fever to be a woman who will give the gift of herself for such a time as this.

Below is a variety of creative ways in which you can join the revolution of mothers by taking The M.O.M. Initiative into the community and using it as a tool for change.

This is a joint ministry venture and your participation is absolutely necessary for the revolution to begin. I want you to know that you don't have to try to figure out how to do this by yourself.

Along with the help and tools provided on our website (www.themominitiative.com), you will also find a Ministry Planning Sheet for several types of ministries where a M.O.M. Group could be effective. Please keep in mind that these are resources to help you. They are creative and practical ways in which you can cultivate relationships in the community and help young mothers see the love of Christ in action. My prayer is that the overflow of your relationship with Jesus will become what your mentee will passionately pursue for herself.

The scope of ministry opportunities is as vast as your God-given imagination. So as you review the various resources below, remember that you have the freedom to begin a M.O.M. Group wherever and however you can.

Please review the list below through the eyes of your community's needs and opportunities. Use what you can. Expand the experience based on your own giftedness, volunteer base and logistics.

Oh! By the way. I'm so glad we're in this together! ☺

Where Can We Begin a M.O.M. Group?

Below are a few venues where you can incorporate a M.O.M. mentor group to impact your church and your community:

- Churches
- Crisis Pregnancy Centers and Homes for Unwed Mothers
- Low Income Apartment Complexes/Neighborhoods
- Homeless Shelters
- Women's Shelters & Crisis Pregnancy Centers
- Juvenile Shelters for Girls
- Prisons

- Community Centers
- Obstetric Departments at Hospitals
- As a Faith-Based Alternative for Court-Directed Parenting Classes
- The Mission Field
- MOPS Groups
- Para-Ministries (MOPS Groups, MOMS International, etc.)
- Schools
- Your Own Home

What Can We Do?

Below is a list of various ways in which you can develop a M.O.M. Group for and from your church, ministry, organization or on your own. You will find a M.O.M. Group Planning Guide for most of the ministries listed above.

M.O.M. Group Planning Guide
In or Through the Local Church

Volunteer Base:
- Leader(s)—M.O.M. Group leader(s)
- Mentor(s)—primary teaching mentor(s)—these may be the M.O.M. Group leader(s)
- Assistant mentor(s)—(optional) assist in planning, calling and preparing snacks
- Mentee(s)—young mother(s) or mother(s)-to-be (no matter how big the M.O.M. Group is, when possible it is best to break off into five mentees per mentor for discussion time)
- K.I.D.s Group leader(s) or childcare team—(optional, but recommended) childcare worker to care for child(ren) of mentors and mentees when necessary

Location:
- Church facilities
- Mentor's home

- Assistant mentor's home
- Local coffee shops
- Restaurants
- Community centers

Format:

Introduction

See the information above to help you begin a M.O.M. Group. You may want to start with a simple M.O.M. Group or you may want to begin with a bang and have a much more structured M.O.M. Group mentoring ministry in your church.

A M.O.M. Group works best when you schedule weekly meetings, and remember, your M.O.M. Group can take place in a classroom, around a table in a conference room, at your dining room table, as a breakfast or lunch meeting, as a play day at the park, or whatever venue works best for you and the moms to whom you are ministering.

If you can, meet your mentee before your M.O.M. Group begins. Give her a copy of *The Making of a Mom* or ask her to purchase it before you meet. Unless you want your first session to be a sweet meet-and-greet time, you may want to have her read the first chapter and answer the questions before you have your first official M.O.M. Group meeting.

M.O.M. Group Time—In the Local Church

- Each session will last one-and-a-half to two hours and will begin with prayer.
- Don't forget the food! Snacks and drinks have a way of making people feel at ease.
- Please be prepared to review the questions found at the end of each chapter, as well as using personal examples.
- Be sure to give yourself time to get to know your mentee and keep your eyes and ears open to look for connecting points in your relationship with her and to identify strengths, weaknesses and needs.
- Look for opportunities to minister to your mentees beyond your group time.

- Provide your personal contact information in order to keep it personal.
- Call your mentee at least once a week. Ask how you can pray for her.
- Send your mentee a birthday card or an encouraging card during and beyond your time with her.
- Work to continue your relationship beyond the 10-week M. O.M. Group.
- Get names of friends from your mentee who may benefit from a mentor relationship.

Here's a sample schedule that may work for your M.O.M. Group:

9:00 AM: Opening Prayer/Meet & Greet Icebreakers/ K.I.D.s Group
9:15 AM: Practical Tip Time—Make a Meal/Learn Excel/ Create a Budget
9:45 AM: M.O.M. to Mom Time (Study/Grow/Chat/ Biblical Mommy-hood)
10:30 AM: Snack Food Fest/Chit-chat/Clean-up
10:45 AM: Pick Up Children from K.I.D.s Group

M.O.M. Group Planning Guide
Homeless Shelters—Women's Shelters—
Homes for Unwed Mothers

Volunteer Base:
- Leader(s)—M.O.M. Group leader(s)
- Mentor(s)—primary teaching mentor(s)—these may be the M.O.M. Group leader(s)
- Assistant mentor(s)—(optional) assist in planning, calling and preparing snacks
- Mentee(s)—young mother(s) or mother(s)-to-be (no matter how big the M.O.M. Group is, it is best to break off into five mentees per mentor for discussion time when possible)
- K.I.D.s Group or childcare team—(optional but recommended) childcare worker to care for child(ren) of mentors and mentees if necessary

Location:
- Homeless shelter
- Women's shelter
- Home for unwed mothers
- Church facilities
- Mentor's home
- Assistant mentor's home

Format:
Introduction

After meeting with the shelter (home) staff and getting their approval, you will want to schedule an introductory session. During that time you have the opportunity to put their hearts at ease and break the ice. After you give your mentee(s) *The Making of a Mom*, you can explain the format and have her (them) read the first chapter and answer the questions before you have your first official M.O.M. Group meeting.

M.O.M. Group Time—Homeless Shelters, Women's Shelters, Homes for Unwed Mothers

- Each session will last about 30 minutes to an hour-and-a-half (depending on the limitations) and will begin with prayer.
- Don't forget the food if you are permitted to bring it! Snacks and drinks have a way of making people feel at ease and will be especially appreciated in these venues.
- Please be prepared to review the questions found at the end of each chapter, as well as using personal examples.
- Be sure to give yourself time to get to know your mentee and keep your eyes and ears open to look for connecting points in your relationship with her and to identify strengths, weaknesses and needs.
- Look for opportunities to minister to your mentees beyond your group time.
- Provide personal contact information in order to keep it personal when possible and appropriate.
- If you are able, call your mentee at least once a week. Ask how you can pray for her.

- If possible, send your mentee a birthday card or an encouraging card during and beyond your time with her.
- Work to continue your relationship beyond the 10-week M.O.M. Group. This may be a good opportunity to connect her with your church or a local church near her.
- Get names of friends from your mentee who may benefit from a mentor relationship.

M.O.M. Group Planning Guide
Low-Income Housing Apartments or Neighborhoods

Volunteer Base:
- Leader(s)—M.O.M. Group leader(s)
- Mentor(s)—primary teaching mentor(s)—these may be the M.O.M. Group leader(s)
- Assistant mentor(s)—(optional) assist in planning, calling and preparing snacks
- Mentee(s)—young mother(s) or mother(s)-to-be (no matter how big the M.O.M. Group is, it is best to break off into five mentees per mentor for discussion time when possible)
- K.I.D.s Group or childcare team—(optional, but recommended) childcare worker to care for child(ren) of mentors and mentees if necessary

Location:
- Apartment complex common room
- Mentee's apartment or home
- Neighborhood community center
- Church facilities
- Mentor's home
- Assistant mentor's home

Format:
Introduction
If you would like to hold your M.O.M. Group in a common room or community center, you will need to meet with the apartment complex staff or community center manager and get approval and find out what their requirements are (use of equipment, any costs,

and so on). You will then want to schedule an introductory session with your mentees. During that time you will have the opportunity to put their hearts at ease and break the ice. After you give your mentee(s) *The Making of a Mom*, you can explain the format and have her (them) read the first chapter and answer the questions before you have your first official M.O.M. Group meeting.

M.O.M. Group Time—Low-Income Housing Apartments or Neighborhoods

- Each session will last one-and-a-half to two hours and will begin with prayer.
- Don't forget the food! Snacks and drinks have a way of making people feel at ease.
- Please be prepared to review the questions found at the end of each chapter, as well as using personal examples.
- Be sure to give yourself time to get to know your mentee and keep your eyes and ears open to look for connecting points in your relationship with her and to identify strengths, weaknesses and needs.
- Look for opportunities to minister to your mentees beyond your group time.
- Provide personal contact information in order to keep it personal.
- Call your mentee at least once a week. Ask how you can pray for her.
- Send your mentee a birthday card or an encouraging card during and beyond your time with her.
- Work to continue your relationship beyond the 12-week M.O.M. Group.
- Get names of friends from your mentee who may benefit from a mentor relationship.
- Providing childcare may increase your potential number of mentees and give you the opportunity to also minister to the children.
- You can use our K.I.D.s Group material to help you with the children. If you use something other than the K.I.D.s Group material, please be sure to be prepared to teach biblical stories on the children's level and have

appropriate activities so that you can make the most of
your time with the children.

M.O.M. Group Planning Guide
Prisons or Juvenile Shelters

Volunteer Base:
- Leader(s)—M.O.M. Group leader(s)
- Mentor(s)—primary teaching mentor(s)—you may need
  several mentors depending on the size of the group or
  you may only be able to have one mentor. It depends
  on what the facility will permit, but the more the better
  so that you can be available for some one-on-one time
  if possible.
- Assistant mentor(s)—(optional) assist in planning
- Mentee(s)—young mother(s) or mother(s)-to-be (you may
  be meeting with one, two or just a few mentees or you
  may be in a classroom or cafeteria full of young mothers, depending on the restrictions and how each facility
  allows their inmates to meet with others)

Location:
- Prison or juvenile shelter visiting room
- Prison or juvenile shelter cafeteria or chapel

Format:
Introduction
This will require a more formal presentation to the one in charge
of activities for inmates. After you get that person's approval, you
will want to schedule an introductory session.

After you've been approved and been given a schedule for
visitation times, you will have the opportunity to meet with the
moms and get to know them during your first M.O.M. Group
time. If you are permitted, you can give your mentee(s) a copy
of *The Making of a Mom* and can explain the format of your time
together. If the mentee(s) is (are) able to keep the book, have
her (them) read the first chapter and answer the questions so
that she (they) will be on the same page with you when you

return. Keep in mind that some facilities won't allow inmates to keep the book, so you may have to read the material and try to share it with them and include some questions to help stimulate conversation.

PLEASE NOTE: You will most likely need to be approved for security clearance before you are permitted to enter the facility. Be sure to give yourself the time you need to go through the necessary procedures to be allowed involvement in a prison ministry. You may have to adjust your schedule based on the time the institution allows for visitation or instruction. Some only allow certain groups to go in once or twice a month.

M.O.M. Group Time—Prisons and Juvenile Shelters

- Each session will depend on the facility's restrictions.
- Your time may have to be altered based on facility restrictions. This is where you will have to be flexible. (Oh, by the way, the number one piece of advice given to all missionaries going on the field is . . . *be flexible!*)
- Please be prepared to review the questions found at the end of each chapter, as well as using personal examples.
- Be sure to give yourself time to get to know your mentee and keep your eyes and ears open to look for connecting points in your relationship with her and to identify strengths, weaknesses and needs.
- Look for opportunities to minister to your mentees beyond your group time. You may be able to extend your church's or ministry's reach by getting involved with helping their children who are definitely hurting while their mommas are incarcerated.
- Send your mentee a birthday card or an encouraging note during and beyond your time with her.
- At your discretion, work to continue your relationship beyond the 10-week M.O.M. Group.
- Seek to connect her/them with a ministry or a church when she/they are released. If you have a M.O.M. Group in your local church, be sure to invite your mentee(s) to it or look for a M.O.M. Group where they can plug in after they are released.

M.O.M. Group Planning Guide
In Schools and Obstetric Departments in Hospitals

Volunteer Base:
- Mentor—primary teaching mentor (you may need more than one mentor depending on the number of mentees)
- Assistant mentor—(optional) assist in planning, calling and preparing snacks
- Mentee(s)—young mother(s) or mother(s)-to-be (best to limit it to five mentees per mentor)

Location:
- School classroom
- Playground
- Cafeteria
- Hospital conference room
- Doctor's office

Format:
Introduction
This will require a more professional introduction and explanation as to what a M.O.M. Group is to school principals or departmental managers in the obstetric units of a hospital.

You may have to adjust your time based on the institution's schedule. You will then want to schedule an introductory session. During that time you will have the opportunity to put the moms' hearts at ease and break the ice.

After you give your mentee(s) *The Making of a Mom*, you can explain the format and have her (them) read the first chapter and answer the questions before you have your first official M.O.M. Group meeting.

M.O.M. Group Time—Hospitals and Schools
- Each session will last one-and-a-half to two hours (unless the school or hospital has a different time frame) and will begin with prayer.
- If permitted, don't forget the food! Snacks and drinks have a way of making people feel at ease.

- Please be prepared to review the questions found at the end of each chapter, as well as using personal examples.
- Be sure to give yourself time to get to know your mentee and keep your eyes and ears open to look for connecting points in your relationship with her and to identify strengths, weaknesses and needs.
- Look for opportunities to minister to your mentee beyond your class time.
- Provide personal contact information in order to keep it personal.
- Call your mentee at least once a week. Ask how you can pray for her.
- Send your mentee a birthday card or an encouraging card during and beyond your time with her.
- Work to continue your relationship beyond the eight-week mentoring program.
- Seek to connect them with a ministry or a church close to where they live. ❁

Appendix 5

HOW TO BECOME A CHRISTIAN

Knowing Christ is a person's most important need. We can't fully become who we were created to be until we come to know the One who created us. We were born to ultimately have a forever relationship with the only One who can enable us to live forever. His name is Jesus. He died for you, He died for me and He invites us to have an intimate, eternal relationship with Him. His promise to us is Himself: Christ in us, the hope of glory (see Col. 1:27). We come to Him with all we are and He makes us new. He makes us different. He makes us His.

We trade all we are for all He is and He enters our hearts and we become new creations (see 2 Cor. 5:17)—we become one with Him. He doesn't promise we will no longer experience pain or heartache once we surrender our lives to Him. He doesn't say the road ahead will be easy or that we will never blow it again. What He does promise is His presence in and through everything we go through. He assures us that He will be our peace when life is hard and that He will be our hope when life seems hopeless.

Jesus. He is not only everything we need. He is all we need. If you don't know Him as your Lord and Savior, today you can enter into that forever relationship He died to give you. The following steps will show you how to begin this relationship:

1. Romans 3:23 tells us that we have all sinned and are therefore separated from God:

   For all have sinned and fall short of the glory of God.

2. Romans 6:23 says that because we are sinners by nature and by choice, we have earned the penalty of eternal separation from God. The price for our sin is death:

   For the wages of sin is death.

3. John 3:16-18 tells us that our sin places us under condemnation. Because God loves us and wants us to have a forever relationship with Him, He made a way out of condemnation and that way is through Jesus and what Jesus accomplished on the cross. Jesus took our sin and shame upon Himself when He died for you and for me:

> For God so loved the world, that he gave his only begotten Son, that whoever believes in Him should not perish but have everlasting life. For God did not send His Son into the world to condemn the world, but that the world through Him might be saved. He who believes in Him is not condemned; but he who does not believe is condemned already, because he has not believed in the name of the only begotten Son of God.

4. Romans 5:8 tells us that we didn't do anything to deserve His love. He just loves us. We are the object of His affection and even when we were separated from Him by sin, He loves us so much that He sent His Son to die for us. What great love the Father has for us:

> But God shows his love for us in that while we were still sinners, Christ died for us (*ESV*).

5. Second Corinthians 5:21 tells us that the great exchange took place on the cross. When we receive Jesus as Lord and Savior, that great exchange is applied to our lives: our sin for His righteousness, our death for His eternal life:

> For our sake he made him to be sin who knew no sin, so that in him we might become the righteousness of God (*ESV*).

6. First Peter 3:18 tells us that, on the cross, Jesus was forsaken by God so that we would never have to be. It was Jesus' willingness to make that exchange by going to the cross that makes a right relationship with God possible for us:

> For Christ also suffered once for sins, the righ-
> teous for the unrighteous, that he might bring
> us to God, being put to death in the flesh but
> made alive in the spirit (*ESV*).

7. Acts 4:12 shows us that Jesus is the way to a relationship
   with God the Father. There is no other way:

   > And there is salvation in no one else, for there is
   > no other name under heaven given among men
   > by which we must be saved (*ESV*).

8. Ephesians 2:8-10 tells us that salvation is only possible
   because of what Jesus did on the cross and through the
   resurrection. We cannot do anything to earn our salvation. God saves us by His grace through faith in Christ
   and the finished work of the cross. When we receive
   Christ, we begin to fulfill the plan He has for our lives
   and we can do the works He calls us to:

   > For by grace you have been saved through faith.
   > And this is not your own doing; it is the gift of
   > God, not a result of works, so that no one may
   > boast. For we are his workmanship, created in
   > Christ Jesus for good works, which God pre-
   > pared beforehand, that we should walk in them
   > (*ESV*).

9. Acts 3:19 tells us that we have to be willing to turn
   from our sins and turn to God. The Bible calls this
   repentance:

   > Now repent of your sins and turn to God, so
   > that your sins may be wiped away (*NLT*).

10. Romans 10:9-10,13 shows us that when we call upon
    the Lord with a heart willing to turn away from our sins
    and follow Him, He saves us from our sins:

> If you confess with your mouth that Jesus is Lord
> and believe in your heart that God raised him from
> the dead, you will be saved. For with the heart one
> believes and is justified, and with the mouth one
> confesses and is saved. . . . For "everyone who calls
> on the name of the Lord will be saved" (*ESV*).

* * *

For years I lived my life the way I wanted to: trying to find happiness; trying to find love—but everything I tried made me feel emptier than before. We all have a place in our hearts that was meant for God alone. That's why we keep looking for ways to feel complete, significant and loved. But the only way we will ever have peace, joy, significance and the love we long for is when we give our lives to Christ and He fills that place in our heart that was created just for Him.

My prayer is that if you don't know Jesus, today you will give your life to Him and discover the love you've been looking for all your life. It's why He died: because He loves you and wants you to be with Him forever. No one else will ever love you like that. Won't you trust Him with your eternity today?

Your next step will be to be baptized. I want to encourage you to find a strong Bible-believing church that can help you in your journey as a Christian.

Oh, and sweet friend, I would love to hear from you if you receive Christ. You can email me at stephanie@themominitiative.com.

❁ ACKNOWLEDGMENTS

The greatest gratitude, without question, goes to You, Jesus. Lord, I still can't believe You saved me and that You would allow me to get in on anything You are doing on this planet. Thank You so much for entrusting me with something You know I'm not capable of doing on my own, and for being with me every step of the way! You wow me and I absolutely *love* the way You love me!

A very special thanks goes to my agent, Blythe Daniel, and to the publishing director at Regal, Kim Bangs. Both of you are amazing women with big hearts for God who are relentlessly serving Christ with passion. You inspire me! How grateful I am that when I shared with you the vision to change our communities and this culture for Christ through missional mentoring, you got it. You really got it!

To my hubby, Donald, I am forever grateful and still deeply in love with you. We all need someone who will believe in us even when we don't believe in ourselves—someone who will pray for us like no one else will and who will encourage us to press on even when we feel like we can't take another step or write another word or organize another event. Donald, you are that and *so* much more to me. You are my biggest cheerleader (without the pompoms, of course), my most consistent prayer warrior and my best friend. I'm blown away that I get to do life with you! I love you like crazy... to the moon and back!

To my sons, Karl and DJ. I *love* being your mom and I'm so honored that God would grant me the privilege of raising you. I couldn't have written this book without you. You were the ones who bore the brunt of every mommy-hood mistake I made. Familiar stories of our lives together are tucked in the pages of this book. You will always be precious gifts to me and I have loved every second of being your mom! Yup! Even the tough ones.

A big thank-you to every M.O.M. from The M.O.M. Initiative team and to every sweet friend who has willingly shared her story and poured out encouragement to those who will read this book while in the hard places of their own mom journey. Through your generosity and transparency, moms are encouraged and lives are changed.

To the entire M.O.M. team: What an amazing group of women who believe as I do that if the hand that rocks the cradle rules the world, then the church that mentors those hands will win it. Thanks for giving of yourselves to pour into the lives of moms and mentors. Thanks for coming together to leave a legacy of faith for those who will come behind us. You have been with me through much of this journey. You are family to me—sisters who give us a little glimpse of what heaven looks like through the relationships we have. You are dear to me and I am so honored to partner with each of you in the ministry.

We all know that books don't just happen. Many hearts and hands go into writing and publishing a book. It might not take a village, but it takes an amazing team. I owe a great debt of gratitude to the publishing board, editors, graphic designers, marketing team, sales staff and everyone involved! Thank you for being in this with me as we serve the Lord together for such a time as this.

To my mom and my birth mom: How could I possibly write about being a mom without you? Even though you both may be with Jesus now, you are forever embedded in my heart. Few people have two mothers who love them so deeply. Thank you, Mom, for loving enough to give me up. Thank you, Mom, for loving me as your own. Thank you both for teaching me that nothing is impossible with God.

And finally, to each precious mom, mentor and ministry leader who reads this: You've been on my heart and mind for years! I don't even have words to explain the profound impact you have had on my life, but I want you to know that every word on the pages of this book was written because you are all so dear to me.

I made a lot of mistakes in my journey through motherhood. One of the biggest ones was going it alone. *The Making of a Mom* and The M.O.M. Initiative exist so that you won't have to do the same. And I can't wait to hear about how you have joined hearts and hands to take your mom journey together! ❁

❁ ABOUT STEPHANIE SHOTT

For more than 25 years, Stephanie has been leading women to live full, fearless and faithful lives. Stephanie is an author, an international speaker and founder of The M.O.M. Initiative, a ministry devoted to helping the Body of Christ make mentoring missional.

Stephanie's life story has given her a unique perspective from which to minister hope and healing to the hearts of women. She was conceived as the result of a rape, survived a decade of abuse, experienced life as a teen mom and as a single mom, and has faithfully and passionately poured her life into women since the day the Lord saved her and changed her in 1987.

She is a pastor's wife, mom and an *abuela* (grandma), who lives in Florida and loves making trips to her home away from home, Costa Rica, where she and her husband served as missionaries for years. When Stephanie is not writing, speaking or serving through The M.O.M. Initiative, you can find her at the beach soaking up the sun with sand between her toes, enjoying game night with her kids, drinking coffee with friends, or hanging out with her hubby.

To find out how you can have Stephanie speak at your next event, how to begin a mentor ministry or a M.O.M. Group, or other topics, you can visit her website at www.stephanieshott.com or email her at stephanie@themominitiative.com.

You can also connect with Stephanie on Facebook at www.facebook.com/StephanieShottAuthor and Twitter at @StephanieShott.

Heartwarming
Resources for Moms

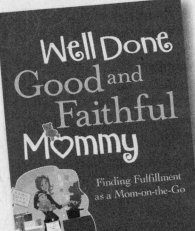

Well Done, Good and Faithful Mommy
Megan Breedlove

Before Megan became a mom, she knew parenting would be easy—and always rewarding. But when her first baby arrived, that bubble quickly burst. If you're like Megan, you've discovered that being a mom is tougher than it looks—and most of the time nobody notices what an incredible job you're doing! *Well Done, Good and Faithful Mommy* will show you how significant you really are—according to God, who always notices and never forgets to say so. You matter, Mommy … far more than you realize.

Manna for Moms
Megan Breedlove

Between diaper changes, carpools, meals and spills, you probably wonder if it's possible to find quality time with God. If only you could connect with your Creator and vacuum cereal out of the car seat at the same time. Megan Breedlove, a mom of five energetic little ones, has discovered the secret: Recognize He is there in every messy, miraculous moment. *Manna for Moms* is a devotional that will inspire you to look up and lighten up—even when you're cleaning up!

Available wherever books are sold!